burgers

burgers

50 recipes celebrating an american classic

rebecca bent

with tom steele

clarkson potter/publishers
new york

For my daughters, Sienna Eve and Ava
Jane, my mini sous chefs, and my husband,
Bruce, for eating everything we dish out.

Copyright © 2004 by Rebecca Gareis-Bent
Photographs copyright by Ben Fink

Published by Clarkson Potter/Publishers,
New York, New York.
Member of the Crown Publishing Group,
a division of Random House, Inc.
www.randomhouse.com

CLARKSON N. POTTER is a trademark and
POTTER and colophon are registered trademarks
of Random House, Inc.

Printed in Singapore

Design by Jan Derevjanik

Library of Congress Cataloging-in-Publication Data
Bent, Rebecca.
Burgers / Rebecca Bent with Tom Steele.
     p.   cm.
Includes bibliographical references and index.
1. Cookery (Meat)   2. Hamburgers.   I. Steele,
Tom.   II. Title.
TX749.G33   2004
641.6'6—dc21   2003013652

ISBN 1-4000-5165-7

10 9 8 7 6 5 4 3 2 1

First Edition

contents

introduction

I have vivid childhood memories

of my Sicilian grandmother, Josephine Concetta, known to all as Monga, hovering over a hot stove, making her beloved "meatballs and gravy." Whenever she finished making a huge batch of her masterpiece, she would saw off the tops of plastic half-gallon milk cartons and fill them to the rim with her specialty so she could dole out portions to relatives to take home. I would sit at Monga's feet and watch as she shouted instructions.

When my mother and aunt joined in to help, I learned that food meant family and relying on one another. So naturally, when I had children of my own, I too brought them right into the kitchen to experience the wonders of cookery.

I first began experimenting with burgers shortly after I got married. When my husband lovingly let me know that his expectations were fairly high, I called on my grandmother and older brother, John Jr., a graduate of the Culinary Institute of America, to help me. During one lesson, my brother concocted a gourmet burger that left my husband speechless. I immediately wanted to learn more about how a plain, ordinary burger could be turned into something of such high culinary standing.

That set off a chain reaction: Every night I invented a new burger recipe, each more sumptuous and decadent—and unusual—than the last. I began writing down my recipes. And I discovered that hamburgers are truly the blue jeans of comfort food. Whether you're in denim overalls or Dolce & Gabbana jeans, you're comfortable and cozy. You can accessorize or not, depending on the occasion. Best of all, jeans are familiar and beloved by the young and old. And so are burgers: You can dress them up and you can take them anywhere. They *have* gotten fabulous makeovers—this book showcases some of the infinite variety—and are hitting the runways of upscale restaurants all over the world, still in the guise of comfort food. There's no reason that such creations can't come out of your own kitchen for your friends and family, on weeknights or for special occasions. Whether in the denim-overall or designer-jean style, burgers are America's most beloved and convenient meal.

For many of the designer style, I am deeply grateful to the accomplished chefs who so graciously contributed special recipes to *Burgers;* you'll find them interwoven throughout the book. Some, like David Waltuck's intriguing Venison Burger au Poivre or Jonathan Waxman's tempting Bacon Burger with ginger, garlic, soy, and sherry, are fairly simple; others are complex and unusual, like Claude Troisgros's sumptuous Foie Gras Burger. All are supremely delicious.

So put on your jeans, and let's cook some burgers.

how to cook a burger

the basic rules

do's

- Be sure to keep your hands impeccably clean while handling raw meats. Wash before, during, and after, preferably with antibacterial soap.

- Burgers are best served on fresh warm or toasted bread. Place the burger on the bread right before you serve it to avoid soggy bread.

- After you've finished cooking but before cutting it in half or serving, let your burger sit for a minute or two to redistribute the juices.

- Patty materials—that is, the "ham" in the burger—can often be substituted. I can only vouch for the way the recipe is written, but feel free to experiment. Cooking times will probably need adjusting if meats are substituted; see "Doneness."

- Grilling burgers outdoors is not only a delicious cooking method, it's an American tradition. But cooking burgers in a skillet produces juicier burgers, because the patties cook in their own juices, instead of those juices dripping away through your grill grate.

- Season a burger with salt *before* cooking, or the salt crystals may not dissolve.

- Always use the freshest ingredients possible.

don'ts

- Never press on a burger with a spatula while it cooks—you'll push out its flavorful juices.

- Never leave a burger unattended while cooking, especially leaner burgers, which can quickly turn into hockey pucks.

doneness

The U.S. Department of Agriculture recommends cooking ground meats to an internal temperature of 160°F., with poultry cooked to 165°F. Take the burger's temperature with a meat thermometer inserted into the thickest part of the burger, the heat sensor (indentations on the stem of the thermometer) in the center of the burger. If the burger is thin, insert the thermometer sideways.

With all due respect to the USDA, some of the recipes in this book take a walk on the rare side. Proceed according to your own preferences and good judgment.

Grinding or chopping your own meat, poultry, or fish ensures the freshest, safest, and least-handled product. Using a meat grinder, electric or hand-cranked, yields the smoothest results, but you can also pulse 1-inch chunks of meat or poultry in the work bowl of a food processor fitted with the metal blade. Be careful not to overprocess, however, or you'll end up with a pasty substance instead of ground meat.

ground beef (1-inch patties)

outdoor grill • Prepare a medium-hot fire, and place the grill rack 4 inches from the coals. Sear the burger for 1 minute, then cover the grill. Halfway through cooking, turn, sear for 1 minute, cover, and cook to desired doneness:

- Rare: 3½ minutes per side
- Medium-rare: 4 minutes per side
- Medium: 4½ minutes per side
- Well-done: 5½ minutes per side

skillet stovetop grilling • Set a heavy skillet, preferably cast iron, over high heat. Add the burgers and cook, turning once. A splatter screen will come in handy to keep the mess to a minimum.

- Rare: 3½ minutes per side
- Medium-rare: 4½ minutes per side
- Medium: 5½ minutes per side
- Well-done: 7½ minutes per side

ground lamb (¾-inch patties)

outdoor grill • Prepare a medium-hot fire in the grill. Place a greased grill rack 4 inches from the coals and grill the lamb burger, turning once.

- Rare: 3 to 4 minutes per side
- Medium-rare: 4 to 4½ minutes per side
- Medium: 5 to 6 minutes per side
- Well-done: 6 to 7 minutes per side

skillet stovetop grilling • Set a heavy skillet, lightly oiled and preferably cast iron, over medium-high heat. Cook the burgers on both sides, turning once.

- Rare: 3 to 4 minutes per side
- Medium-rare: 4 to 4½ minutes per side
- Medium: 5 to 6 minutes per side
- Well-done: 6 to 7 minutes per side

ground pork

Ground pork patties, ½ inch in thickness, need 8 to 10 minutes of medium-high heat to cook through, whether on an outdoor grill or in a grill pan.

ground game

Ground buffalo and venison are so low in fat that they should be cooked no longer than 4 minutes per side, and the burgers should be *at least* ½-inch thick. The outdoor grill should be medium-hot, with the grill rack 4 inches from the hot coals. For skillet stovetop grilling, a heavy skillet, lightly oiled and preferably cast iron, should be set over high heat and, again, the burger cooked no more than 4 minutes per side.

ground poultry

Ground chicken and turkey need to be cooked through for safety purposes. The outdoor grill should be hot, the lightly oiled grill rack 4 inches from the coals, and the poultry patties ¾-inch thick. Grill the patties for 5 minutes per side. To pan-fry ¾-inch-thick patties, add enough oil to film a heavy skillet and place over medium-high heat. Fry the patties until well-done, 7 minutes per side.

beef burgers

There are times when nothing will satisfy a craving for comfort like a gigantic, succulent burger. Beef is by far the most popular patty, and probably the one you grew up on. This chapter includes a wide range of variations, from the very simple, such as my Big Juicy Butter Burger, to the highly sophisticated, like Dean Fearing's Mansion Roadhouse Burger with Tobacco Onions.

geoffrey zakarian's town burger

This recipe comes from the hip, critically acclaimed restaurant Town, nestled below the Chambers Hotel in midtown Manhattan. Executive chef and owner Geoffrey Zakarian created this straightforwardly delicious burger to satisfy the demands of his lunch regulars. Serve with Town Gingered Cole Slaw (page 86) and Town Buttered Chips (page 78).

serves 4

- 1 to 2 tablespoons olive oil (to season grill or skillet)
- 4 8-ounce prepackaged organic prime ground beef patties
- 1 teaspoon kosher salt
- ½ teaspoon freshly ground black pepper
- 1 tablespoon salted butter
- 1 tablespoon chopped parsley
- 4 English muffins, preferably Wolferman's
- 4 thick slices of beefsteak tomato

Preheat a grill or cast-iron skillet, wiping down the grate or the skillet with olive oil before heating over medium-high flame.

Season the hamburgers generously on both sides with the salt and pepper. Char the burgers well on both sides: about 4 minutes per side on the grill, 4½ minutes per side in a skillet.

Just before the burgers reach the desired temperature, remove them to a rack to rest. Divide the butter evenly on top of each burger and sprinkle with a little chopped parsley. While the burgers are resting, grill or toast each of the split English muffins. After 5 minutes, return the burgers to the grill or skillet to heat through before serving.

Place a burger on each of 4 English muffin halves, top with tomato and the other half of the muffin, and serve.

chili burger

I once visited a buffalo farm in Pennsylvania with a former president of the Culinary Institute of America. He gave me several pounds of buffalo chili to take home and sample. I fell in love with the wonderful rustic flavor and felt obliged to convert the chili recipe into this burger.

serves 4

- 1 to 2 tablespoons olive oil (to season grill or skillet)
- 2 pounds lean ground beef sirloin
- 1 garlic clove, finely chopped
- ½ red onion, finely chopped
- ¼ green bell pepper, stemmed, seeded, and diced
- ¼ teaspoon red pepper flakes
- 1 teaspoon celery salt
- 1 teaspoon ground cumin
- 1 teaspoon ground nutmeg
- 1 teaspoon dried oregano
- 1 tablespoon (packed) dark brown sugar
- 1 tablespoon canned tomato sauce, or 1½ teaspoons each tomato paste and water
- 4 fresh basil leaves, finely chopped
- 1 tablespoon ketchup
- 2 tablespoons kidney beans
- 4 English muffins, split and toasted
- 2 tablespoons unsalted butter, at room temperature

Preheat a grill or cast-iron skillet, wiping down the grate or the skillet with olive oil before heating over medium-high flame.

In a large bowl, combine the sirloin, garlic, onion, bell pepper, red pepper flakes, celery salt, cumin, nutmeg, oregano, brown sugar, tomato sauce, basil, and ketchup. With a fork, lightly mash the kidney beans in a small bowl—they should be broken and squished, but not into a smooth puree. Add to the meat mixture, and thoroughly blend with your hands. Divide into 4 patties at least 1-inch thick. Sauté over medium-high heat until medium-rare: 4 minutes per side on the grill, 4½ minutes per side in a skillet.

Butter the toasted English muffins, place a burger in each, and serve.

mini-burgers with waffled white bread

Mini-burgers make perfect party food: Guests can hold them in one hand. Because mini-burger buns are not easily purchased, I place a piece of white bread, crusts trimmed, in a heated nonstick waffle iron, then press down long enough to toast it and leave waffle indentations in the bread. One slice of bread provides buns for about four mini-burgers.

serves 4

- **3 pieces sliced white sandwich bread, crusts removed**
- **9 ounces ground beef (a little over ½ pound)**
- **½ teaspoon kosher salt**
- **2 tablespoons chopped parsley, plus 12 sprigs, for garnish**
- **2 tablespoons olive oil (to season skillet), optional**
- **12 thin slices Cheddar cheese, about 2 inches square (optional)**

note: Try topping with other flavors such as fresh herbs, a dab of ketchup, a sliver of roasted bell pepper, or a pinch of ground spice. There are endless possibilities to add more flavor and color to these versatile minis.

Preheat an electric nonstick waffle iron to medium.

Place a slice of trimmed bread in the center of the hot waffle iron and press down hard to toast and perforate the bread for 1 minute, or until the bread's waffle design has browned nicely. When toasted, cut each slice into square pieces about 1 inch by 1 inch. You should have enough bread for about 12 mini-burgers.

In a medium bowl, combine the beef, salt, and chopped parsley, and mix well with your hands. Remove a heaping tablespoon of the mixture—a little less than 1 ounce—and roll it into a ball. Flatten it slightly into a patty no thicker than 1 inch. The 9 ounces of beef should make about 12 mini-burgers.

Warm a cast-iron skillet over medium-high heat. Slick the skillet with the olive oil. Or, if using a grill, cook the mini-burgers on a sheet of aluminum foil perforated several times with a fork to allow the juices to drip away.

Cook the burgers no longer than 1 minute per side for medium-rare. Top each burger with the optional cheese as soon as you flip the burger. Serve each burger between 2 slices of waffled bread, with a sprig of parsley on top (see Note).

michele evans plesser's caribbean jump-up burgers

Michele Evans Plesser won two James Beard Cookbook Awards in 1997 and 2002 for coauthoring *La Cucina Siciliana di Gangivecchio* and its sequel. She has been a mentor to me, and sent me this charming recipe from St. Thomas in the Virgin Islands. In the Caribbean, a "jump-up" is a term for a party, often impromptu, allowing little time for marinating meats, so spicy jerk rubs make the perfect solution. The rub is applied briskly with your palm on the outside of the burger to help the flavors seep in. Try to use whole spices, toasting them when appropriate and grinding them yourself, either in a mortar and pestle or a spice grinder.

serves 4

for the jerk rub

- ½ **teaspoon kosher salt**
- ½ **teaspoon freshly ground black pepper**
- ½ **teaspoon freshly ground dried allspice berries (called pimento in Jamaica, after the tree that produces allspice)**
- ½ **teaspoon garlic salt**
- ½ **teaspoon onion salt**
- ⅛ **teaspoon ground cinnamon**
- ⅛ **teaspoon ground nutmeg (or freshly grated)**

for the burgers

- 1 **to 2 tablespoons olive oil (to season grill or skillet)**
- 1 **pound ground beef sirloin**
- ½ **pound ground beef chuck**
- ½ **teaspoon dried thyme**
- 4 **hamburger buns, split and toasted**

Combine all the jerk ingredients well in a bowl.

Preheat a grill or cast-iron skillet, wiping down the grate or the skillet with olive oil before heating over a medium-high flame.

In a large bowl, gently combine the sirloin, chuck, and thyme. Divide into 4 firm patties at least 1-inch thick and set aside. Coat each side of the burgers with equal amounts of the jerk rub by turning each burger in the bowl. Rub with the palm of your hand to press in the mixture slightly.

Cook the burgers over medium-high heat until medium-rare: 4 minutes per side on the grill, 4½ minutes per side in a skillet. Serve on toasted hamburger buns.

coconut-flake hawaiian burger

This exotic burger served with tropical Coco-Mac Nut Glaze is perfect for any occasion, with its fanciful combination of coconut, beef, and macadamia nut. This recipe is certain to surprise and please.

serves 4

1 to 2 tablespoons olive oil (to season grill or skillet)

2 pounds ground beef sirloin

½ teaspoon kosher salt

½ teaspoon freshly ground black pepper

2 tablespoons (packed) dark brown sugar

1 tablespoon coconut flakes

3 tablespoons coconut cream, such as Coco Lopez

   Coco-Mac Nut Glaze (recipe follows)

8 slices peasant bread, toasted

2 ounces pineapple chunks in juice, drained and diced

Preheat a grill or cast-iron skillet, wiping down the grate or the skillet with olive oil before heating over a medium-high flame.

In a bowl, blend the sirloin, salt, pepper, brown sugar, coconut flakes, and coconut cream, and mix well. Divide into 4 patties at least 1-inch thick. Cook over medium-high heat until medium-rare: 4 minutes per side on the grill, 4½ minutes per side in a skillet. Remove from the heat and smear with warm Coco-Mac Nut Glaze. Serve on toasted peasant bread, with diced pineapples on the side.

coco-mac nut glaze

1 tablespoon unsalted butter

8 macadamia nuts, ground to a powdery consistency in a mini-processor or spice grinder

1 tablespoon coconut flakes

3 tablespoons coconut cream, such as Coco Lopez

Place all ingredients in a saucepan and cook over medium heat, stirring, until thick, about 5 minutes.

corner bistro burger with my fried parsley

Corner Bistro is legendary for serving its loosely packed, 9-ounce, juicy burgers at friendly prices until 3 o'clock each morning, in an unpretentious Greenwich Village pub setting. Superstar chefs Mario Batali and David Waltuck told *New York* magazine that Corner Bistro serves their favorite burger. The Bistro's owner, Bill O'Donnell, maintains that "there are no secrets" to his burgers' success. Corner Bistro uses a salamander, a long iron rod with a cast-iron disc at one end and a wooden handle at the other. The disc is heated over a burner until it's red-hot, then it's passed over the burger, browning it quickly. Since most homes don't have salamanders, I converted this recipe for an oven broiler. I also include my own recipe for fried parsley, a great condiment.

serves 4

for the burgers

- 2¼ **pounds 85% lean ground choice beef chuck, loosely packed**
- 4 **English muffins, split and toasted**

for the fried parsley

About 2 cups vegetable oil, enough to fill your pot to a depth of 1 inch (or, if using a deep fryer, follow manufacturer's recommendations)

- 1½ **cups packed curly-leaf parsley, leaves only, stems discarded, rinsed and spun-dry completely**

Kosher salt

Preheat a broiler and place the rack 6 inches away from the heat. Form 4 loosely packed patties, ¾ inch thick, and place them on a broiler pan. Broil the burgers on the first side for about 2 minutes, flip, and continue to cook for about 1½ minutes for medium-rare. Watch the burgers carefully to avoid burning. If you have a small broiler, cook 2 at a time.

Pour the vegetable oil into a deep, heavy pot. Heat over a medium-low flame until a deep-frying or candy thermometer reaches 350°F. (If you don't have a thermometer, see page 77.) Carefully add the parsley leaves, using a splatter screen if you have one, because the oil may splatter. Gently swirl the skillet to ensure even frying. Fry for 2 to 3 minutes, or until lightly crispy. Remove from the heat before removing the parsley with a slotted spoon. Drain on paper towels and sprinkle with kosher salt.

To serve: Place each burger on a toasted English muffin, and top with fried parsley and the muffin top.

americana burger with huevos fritos

A good friend of the family is from Ecuador, and she happily loaned me a cookbook that her sister mailed her from Quito. *¡Gracias, Anita y Yolanda, la hamburguesa es deliciosa!*

serves 4

- 1 to 2 tablespoons olive oil (to season grill or skillet)
- 1 medium white onion, minced
- 2 garlic cloves, minced
- ½ cup dry red wine, such as merlot
- 1 pound ground pork
- 1 pound ground beef chuck
- 1 cup olive oil, for frying
- 4 large eggs
- 1 teaspoon kosher salt
- ½ teaspoon freshly ground black pepper
- 8 pieces of thinly sliced toast, or 4 pieces for open-faced burgers

Preheat a grill or cast-iron skillet, wiping down the grate or the skillet with olive oil before heating over a medium-high flame.

In a sauté pan, combine the onion and garlic with the red wine. Cook until the onion is soft and the wine has evaporated, about 10 minutes. Remove the pan from the heat and set aside to cool. Scrape the onion mixture into a large bowl, add the ground pork and ground beef, and mix well. Form into 4 patties and set aside in the refrigerator for about 15 minutes.

Pour the 1 cup of olive oil into a skillet and place over medium heat. Add the eggs and cover the pan at once; the hot oil may splatter. Swirl the pan gently to make sure the hot oil reaches the tops of the eggs. Let the eggs fry for 1 minute, or until just cooked through. Remove from the heat and set aside. Do not try to remove the hot fried eggs immediately; wait until the oil has stopped popping, then carefully remove the eggs and drain them on paper towels. Sprinkle with a bit of salt and pepper.

Meanwhile, place the burgers on the hot grill or skillet and cook through, about 5 minutes per side. Remove and serve on toast with the egg atop the burger. These can be eaten open-faced or between 2 pieces of toast.

the telepans' hungarian hamburger

For over five years, Bill Telepan has run the kitchen of the exalted JUdson Grill in mid-town Manhattan. The dishes on his greenmarket-driven menus are breathtakingly direct and deeply flavored. When we asked Bill for a burger recipe, he called his mother, Evelyn, for his favorite childhood recipe, which she called "Hungarian hamburgers." These are straightforward, old-fashioned, and mighty delicious.

serves 4 to 8 (it's easy to eat 2!)

2 **day-old kaiser rolls**

1 **pound ground pork**

1 **large egg**

1 **medium onion, finely grated**

2 **tablespoons chopped flat-leaf parsley**

1 **teaspoon kosher salt**

½ **teaspoon freshly ground black pepper**

½ **cup vegetable oil or, preferably, fresh lard**

8 **fresh poppy seed kaiser rolls, split**
   Ketchup, for serving

Without removing the crusts, tear the day-old kaiser rolls into small pieces. Place in a medium bowl, cover the pieces with about 4 cups of warm water, and soak until very moist, about 10 minutes. Squeeze out the liquid. In a large bowl, combine the moistened bread with the pork, egg, onion, parsley, salt, and pepper. Mix well. Divide the mixture into 8 burgers, each about ¼ inch thick.

Heat the oil or lard in a large skillet over a medium flame until it shimmers. Fry the burgers in 2 batches, browning them on both sides for 15 minutes per side; pork must be fully cooked. Serve 1 (or 2) burgers tucked into split fresh kaiser rolls, and pass the ketchup separately.

jonathan waxman's bacon burger with onion rings

Jonathan Waxman was among the most celebrated chefs in the country during the 1980s, when he was instrumental in popularizing lighter menus driven by fresh ingredients—what became known as California cuisine. He is now owner and executive chef at Washington Park on a posh stretch of lower Fifth Avenue in Greenwich Village, where he serves this easy-to-prepare, intensely flavorful bacon burger.

serves 4

for the burgers

- **1 to 2 tablespoons olive oil (to season grill or skillet)**
- **3 pounds ground choice beef chuck (80% lean)**
- **1 teaspoon grated fresh ginger**
- **2 garlic cloves, minced**
- **1 tablespoon soy sauce**
- **2 tablespoons fino sherry or dry red wine**
- **1 shallot, peeled and minced**
- **1 teaspoon kosher salt**
- **½ teaspoon freshly ground black pepper**
- **4 burger buns**
- **1 pound sliced bacon, fried crisply and drained on paper towels**

Preheat a grill or cast-iron skillet, wiping down the grate or the skillet with olive oil before heating over a medium-high flame.

Place the chuck in a large bowl. Add the ginger, garlic, soy sauce, sherry, shallot, salt, and pepper, and mix lightly. Form 4 plump patties and set aside while you prepare the onion rings.

Make the Onion Rings: Place the flour in a medium bowl. Pour the wine into the flour and whisk until the flour dissolves; the consistency should be somewhat creamy.

In a large, deep skillet or Dutch oven, heat the oil to 325°F. (Without a fryer or candy thermometer, see page 77.) To help the slurry stick to the onions, make sure to sprinkle them with a drop of flour. Dip the flour-covered onion rings into the flour-wine slurry and coat well. Fry for 5 minutes, occasionally turning with tongs, until golden. Drain on a plate lined with paper towels and season with salt to taste.

for the onion rings

1 cup all-purpose flour, plus ¼ cup flour

1 cup white wine

4 large sweet onions, peeled and cut into 1-inch-thick rings

1 quart peanut or corn oil

Kosher salt

Cook the burgers to desired doneness: about 3 minutes per side on grill, 3½ minutes per side in a skillet. Place on the bottom buns, and divide the bacon among them. Cover with the top buns and serve with plenty of onion rings.

chocolate-encrusted cranberry burger

Don't shy away from this intriguing (and admittedly peculiar-sounding) combination of chocolate and berries. This burger should be cooked only on a grill (inside on a ridged grill pan or outside on a charcoal or gas grill), because the brown sugar will burn in a flat pan. This burger-coating method is a favorite of mine because it is easy to prepare, yet the taste suggests you've been working at it for hours.

serves 4

for the crust

- ¼ **teaspoon kosher salt**
- 2 **packages (about 1.25 ounces each) powdered hot chocolate mix, such as Hershey's or Jacques Torres**
- ½ **cup (packed) light brown sugar (see Note)**
- 1 **pinch chili powder, or 1 tablespoon if you like a spicy kick**

for the burger

- 1 **to 2 tablespoons olive oil (to season grill or skillet)**
- 1 **cup canned whole-berry cranberry sauce (half as topping, half for the patty)**
- 2 **pounds ground beef chuck**
- ¼ **cup finely chopped fresh mint leaves**
- 1 **teaspoon kosher salt**
- ½ **teaspoon freshly ground black pepper**
- 4 **sourdough rolls, sliced and toasted**

In a large shallow bowl, blend all the crust ingredients.

Preheat a grill or ridged cast-iron skillet, wiping down the grate or the skillet with olive oil before heating over a medium-high flame.

Mash ½ cup of the cranberry sauce, and strain off and discard the liquid.

In a separate bowl, combine the ground beef, mint, mashed cranberries, salt, and pepper. Form into 4 equal patties, and flatten slightly until the burgers are about 1 inch thick. Place one burger at a time in the crust mixture and flip until the outside of the patty is completely coated and none of the beef is visible though the coating. Set aside for 5 minutes.

Cook the coated burgers over medium-high heat until medium-rare: 4 minutes per side on the grill, 4½ minutes per side in a ridged skillet. Serve on split toasted sourdough rolls with the remaining ½ cup of cranberry sauce on top of the burger.

variations

While in school at the French Culinary Institute, I attended a baking lecture by Jacques Torres. When I told him about this burger, he smiled and said, "Wow, like I always say, chocolate is great on everything." And you know what, he's right.

This burger has other coating possibilities:

- ½ cup (packed) dark brown sugar mixed well with ½ cup chili powder. This is a great combination from my older brother, a professional chef (and he never lets me forget it).

- ½ cup (packed) brown sugar blended with 2 tablespoons cinnamon. I call this "Mom's After-School Burger"—comfort food at its best!

note: Since there is brown sugar in this recipe, open grates over a flame will most likely flare up from time to time (this is fun, but keep children away!), and even after the burger is removed, until the sugar burns off.

roy yamaguchi's mama burger with chopped mushrooms

Convivial Roy Yamaguchi, chef-owner of the original Roy's Restaurant and its many affiliates, has been delighting diners from Honolulu and California to Manhattan since 1988, when he opened his flagship restaurant. Chef Roy's famous Hawaiian fusion dishes use only the freshest ingredients, and reflect his Japanese-Hawaiian heritage. This burger was inspired by his highly popular Mama's Meatloaf recipe. Serve with Roy's Maui Onion Salad (page 85) on the side.

serves 4

for the burgers

- 1 to 2 tablespoons olive oil (to season grill or skillet)
- 1 large egg
- 1 small red bell pepper, finely diced
- 1 small green bell pepper, finely diced
- 1 small celery stalk, finely diced
- 10 white button mushrooms, finely diced
- 2 tablespoons ketchup
- 1 teaspoon kosher salt
- ½ teaspoon freshly ground black pepper
- 2 pounds ground beef chuck
- 1 cup panko (Japanese bread crumbs), or dry white bread crumbs
- 4 hamburger buns, sliced and toasted

for the chopped mushrooms

- 2 tablespoons olive oil
- 3 garlic cloves, minced
- 8 shiitake mushrooms, coarsely chopped
- 8 white button mushrooms, coarsely chopped
- 2 tablespoons unsalted butter
- 1 tablespoon chopped fresh basil
  Salt and freshly ground black pepper to taste

Make the mushrooms: Heat the olive oil over a medium flame in a skillet large enough to hold the chopped mushrooms in a single layer. Add the garlic and cook until golden brown, about 2 minutes. Add the shiitake and button mushrooms. After 5 minutes, they will release their moisture. When that evaporates,

add the butter and toss for another 2 minutes. Add the basil, salt, and pepper. Set aside.

Make the burgers: Slick a grill, a well-seasoned flat griddle, or a large non-stick sauté pan with olive oil, and preheat over a medium-high flame. Beat the egg in a large mixing bowl. Add the red pepper, green pepper, celery, mushrooms, ketchup, salt, and pepper. Add the ground beef and mix thoroughly with your hands. Add the bread crumbs, blend well, and form into 4 patties.

Cook the burgers over medium-high heat until medium-rare: 4 minutes per side on the grill, 4½ minutes per side in a skillet. Serve on a toasted bun topped with the sautéed chopped mushrooms.

mushrooms

Mushrooms should be stored in a paper bag in the refrigerator. Before use, either wipe them down with a damp cloth or rinse them under cold water.

However, if they are quite dirty, just peel off their skins to make it easy.

big juicy butter burger

While I was pulling together the recipes for this book, my editor asked me what I knew about butter burgers. Staring at him blankly, I wondered if he was joking. But after some research I discovered that butter burgers have been served all across America for the last few decades. This recipe is a salute to the restaurants and home cooks who dare to serve this decadent, succulent, butter-stuffed burger in our health-obsessed society.

serves 4

1 to 2 tablespoons olive oil (to season grill or skillet)

2 pounds ground beef round

1 pinch kosher salt

1 pinch freshly ground black pepper

4 tablespoons unsalted butter, softened

4 hamburger rolls, toasted and well buttered

Preheat a grill or cast-iron skillet, wiping down the grate or the skillet with olive oil before heating over a medium-high flame.

In a medium bowl, combine the ground beef, salt, and pepper. Mix well with your hands and form into 8 patties.

Create a small crater in the center of 4 of the patties, leaving about a ¼-inch edge, and place 1 tablespoon of butter in each center. Top with the other patties, pinching the seams together well. Make sure the stuffing is completely covered. Cook the burgers over medium-high heat until medium-rare: 5 minutes per side on the grill, 5½ minutes per side in a skillet. Flip carefully so they don't break open.

variations

Spruce up your butter:

- **Herb Butter:** Combine 4 cloves of roasted garlic (page 81), 3 teaspoons of chopped fresh rosemary, 2 teaspoons of chopped fresh oregano, and 4 tablespoons of softened unsalted butter. Mix well, place in a ramekin, and let the mixture set in the refrigerator for 30 minutes. Stuff burgers by scooping out approximately 1 tablespoon of the mixture per burger.

- **Wisconsin Cheddar and Butter:** Combine ¼ cup of shredded sharp Wisconsin Cheddar with 4 tablespoons of softened unsalted butter. Mix well, place in a ramekin, and let the mixture set in the refrigerator for 30 minutes. Stuff burgers by scooping out approximately 1 tablespoon of mixture per burger.

- **Butter on the Outside:** Instead of stuffing burgers, prepare 4 patties and cook while basting with the Herb or Cheddar Butter mixture, approximately 1 tablespoon per patty.

home of the butter burger

Solly's Grille in Glendale, Wisconsin, has been serving butter burgers since 1936. On a good day, they may sell up to 400 butter burgers. It is no surprise "cooking food with lots of of love and butter" is their slogan.

josé hurtado-prud'homme's mi cocina burger à la mexicana

Mi Cocina, owned by José Hurtado-Prud'homme and his wife Marzena Hurtado, is among the most popular Mexican restaurants in Manhattan. Prud'homme's highly authentic regional Mexican cuisine is personified in this burger, which he tells us takes him back to the aromas of his grandmother's kitchen, north of Mexico City, where he first took to cooking. The burger's smooth flavor is stepped up by the adobo. It becomes even more festive with the addition of Prud'homme's fanciful Salsa Cruda (page 33) and Avocado Ketchup (page 89).

serves 6

for the burgers

- **1 to 2 tablespoons olive oil (to season grill or skillet)**
- **¼ cup onion, chopped into ⅛-inch dice**
- **3 pounds ground beef chuck**
- **3 tablespoons fresh thyme leaves**
- **½ cup José's Adobo (recipe follows)**
- **12 romaine lettuce leaves, cut to fit just over burgers**
- **6 Mexican telera rolls, split, or onion rolls**

Preheat a grill or cast-iron skillet, wiping down the grate or the skillet with olive oil before heating over a medium-high flame.

Rinse the chopped onion in hot water, then plunge into ice water and drain. (This sweetens the onion slightly.)

Mix the beef, onion, thyme, and adobo with your hands until well blended. Divide into 6 patties at least 1 inch thick. Cook the burgers over medium-high heat until medium-rare: 4 minutes per side on the grill, 4½ minutes per side in a skillet.

Serve topped with romaine leaves between slices of telera rolls.

continued on page 32

josé's adobo

3 pieces of guajillo chile
½ teaspoon dried oregano
½ teaspoon dried thyme
¼ teaspoon cumin powder
1 garlic clove, peeled
1 tablespoon olive oil

Lightly toast the guajillos in a dry cast-iron skillet over medium heat, then soak in hot water for 10 minutes. Drain well.

In a blender, purée the toasted chiles with 1 cup water, the oregano, thyme, cumin, and garlic. In a small saucepan, heat the oil over a medium flame, add the puréed chile mixture, and simmer, stirring, for about 3 minutes. Transfer to a glass container and let cool.

note: Guajillo peppers are mildly hot dried red chiles, about 4 inches long and reddish brown in color. Ancho chiles are somewhat easier to find, and may be substituted.

josé's salsa cruda

In some counties, *La Salsa* is a dance. However, for our purposes, salsa is a combination of chopped vegetables, such as tomato and onion, with some kind of chile pepper, such as jalapeño or Anaheim. This recipe is great for burgers but can also be served on fish, beef, or pork chops.

serves 6

2½ **cups tomatoes, chopped into ¼-inch dice**

½ **cup red onion, chopped into ⅛-inch dice**

1 **jalapeño, stemmed, seeded, and finely chopped**

1 **tablespoon capers, rinsed and drained**

1 **tablespoon freshly squeezed lime juice (from about ½ lime)**

2 **tablespoons olive oil**

   Salt to taste

¼ **cup roughly chopped fresh cilantro**

Mix all ingredients together, adding the cilantro leaves just before serving. This can be served immediately; however, allowing the salsa to chill before serving and adding the cilantro at the last minute makes it especially fresh-tasting—a nice treat on a hot day.

cheeseburgers

Long live cheese! With such contributions as grill master Bobby Flay's Mesa Grill Burger with Double Cheddar Cheese, Grilled Vidalia Onion and Horseradish Mustard, and the indulgent Five-Cheese Burger with Pears and Walnuts, this chapter takes the cheeseburger to new heights.

five-cheese burger
with pears and walnuts

This burger blends a variety of cheeses, resulting in an elegant but zesty flavor. The recipe is flexible: Mix and match your own cheese blends to create something you can call your own. If you're having a party, keep the grated cheeses separate and allow guests to select their own combinations.

serves 4

- 1 to 2 tablespoons olive oil (to season grill or skillet)
- 2 pounds ground beef round or chuck
- 1 teaspoon kosher salt
- ¼ teaspoon freshly ground black pepper
- 1 teaspoon finely chopped fresh oregano
- ¼ cup crumbled Gorgonzola
- ¼ cup grated fontina
- ¼ cup grated pecorino Romano
- ½ cup grated mozzarella
- ½ cup ricotta cheese (always use ricotta as a binder, if you choose to mix and match)
- 1 whole pear
- 4 sourdough rolls, split and toasted
- ¼ cup walnuts, finely ground in a spice grinder

Preheat a grill or cast-iron skillet, wiping down the grate or the skillet with olive oil before heating over a medium-high flame.

In a large bowl, combine the beef, salt, pepper, and oregano. Mix well using your hands. Divide into 4 patties at least 1 inch thick. Sauté the burgers over medium-high heat until medium-rare: 4 minutes per side on the grill, 4½ minutes per side in a skillet.

Meanwhile, mix the 5 cheeses until well blended, folding in the ricotta last.

When the burgers are almost done, peel, stem, core, and thinly slice the pear.

A few minutes before removing the burgers from the heat, place an ice cream scoop—or about 3 heaping tablespoons—of the cheese mixture on top of each burger. Flatten the mounds with a spatula and cover the pan or grill to melt the cheese, about 2 minutes.

Serve the burgers on split and toasted sourdough rolls, with a few slices of pear on top of the melted cheese, sprinkled with the ground walnuts.

bobby flay's mesa grill burger with double cheddar cheese

At his flagship restaurant, Mesa Grill, Bobby Flay made New Yorkers—and eventually, everyone else—take Southwestern cuisine seriously. On the Food Network and elsewhere, he brought a new kind of natural charm and estimable culinary talent to grilling and all sorts of other cooking techniques. Here's his succulent Mesa Grill Burger.

serves 4

for the grilled vidalia onion

- 2 **tablespoons olive oil**
- 1 **large Vidalia onion, sliced crosswise into ½-inch slices**
  Salt and freshly ground pepper to taste

for the horseradish mustard

- 1 **cup smooth Dijon mustard**
- 2 **tablespoons prepared horseradish, drained**

for the burger

- 2 **pounds freshly ground beef chuck**
- ¼ **teaspoon kosher salt**
  Pinch of freshly ground black pepper
- 8 **¼-inch-thick slices Cheddar cheese**
- 4 **slices beefsteak tomatoes**
- 4 **romaine lettuce leaves**
- 4 **sesame seed hamburger buns**

Make the grilled onion: Preheat a grill to high.

Brush the 2 tablespoons of olive oil on both sides of the onion slices and season with salt and pepper. Grill for 3 to 4 minutes on each side until golden brown. Set aside.

Make the horseradish mustard: Whisk the mustard and horseradish together in a small bowl until well combined. Set aside.

Form the ground beef into four 8-ounce burgers and season on both sides with salt and pepper. Grill for 3 to 4 minutes on each side for medium. During the last minutes of cooking, add 2 slices of cheese to each burger, cover the grill, and let the cheese melt, about 1 minute. Place the burgers on buns and top with the reserved grilled onions, tomato, lettuce, and a dollop of horseradish mustard.

stuffed blue-cheese burger
with apple and bacon

This burger conjoins some of America's favorite flavors in appetizing harmony: blue cheese, apple, and bacon. The recipe is a bit more labor-intensive than others, but it's well worth the effort. For me, it was an instant hit when my two-year-old daughter gobbled it down without any hesitation. Feel free to experiment with different cheeses: Shredded Swiss, Cheddar, or fontina all work well.

serves 4

- 1 to 2 tablespoons olive oil (to season grill or skillet)
- 8 thick slices apple-smoked bacon
- 2 pounds ground beef chuck
- 1 teaspoon kosher salt
- 1 teaspoon freshly ground black pepper
- 2 teaspoons dried thyme
- 1 teaspoon crumbled dried sage
- ½ cup crumbled blue cheese, preferably Stilton
- 1 Fuji apple
- 4 sesame seed rolls, split and toasted

Preheat a grill or cast-iron skillet, wiping down the grate or the skillet with olive oil before heating over a medium-high flame.

Cook the bacon in a dry skillet over medium heat. When done to your liking, place on paper towels to drain, and set aside.

In a medium bowl, combine the ground beef, salt, pepper, thyme, and sage. Mix well using your hands. Form into 8 thin patties. Create small craters in the center of half of the patties, leaving an edge of about ¼ inch all the way around, and place a scant 2 tablespoons of blue cheese in the center. Top each with another patty, pinching the seams together. Make sure the stuffing is completely covered.

Cook the burgers over medium-high heat until medium-rare: 4 minutes per side on the grill, 4½ minutes per side in a skillet. Be gentle when you turn the burger so that it doesn't break open.

Thinly slice the apple and top each burger with the slices just before removing from the heat. Serve the burgers topped with bacon on the toasted rolls.

left: Stuffed Blue-Cheese Burger with Apple and Bacon

below: Monga's Burger with Lacy Parmesan Crisps and Fried Tomatoes (page 40)

monga's burger with lacy parmesan crisps and fried tomatoes

It took me years of bribing to get this well-coveted recipe from my Sicilian grandmother, Josephine Concetta, known to all as Monga. I added the Parmesan crisps—called *frico,* a specialty of the Friuli region of northern Italy—to soften the tart tomato taste. This burger joins northern and southern Italian cuisine in mouthwatering delight.

serves 4

for the burger

- 1 to 2 tablespoons olive oil (to season grill or skillet)
- 2 pounds ground beef sirloin
- 2 teaspoons minced garlic
- ¼ teaspoon kosher salt
- 1 pinch freshly ground black pepper
- ⅓ cup finely chopped parsley

for the fried tomato

- 1 tablespoon finely chopped fresh rosemary
- 1 cup dried bread crumbs with Italian seasoning
- 1 large, firm tomato, sliced into 4 ½-inch slices
- 2 tablespoons olive oil

Preheat the grill or a cast-iron skillet, wiping down the grate or the skillet with olive oil before heating over a medium-high flame.

In a large bowl, combine the ground sirloin with the garlic, salt, pepper, and parsley. Mix well using your hands. Divide into 4 patties at least 1 inch thick. Cook the burgers over medium-high heat until medium-rare: 4 minutes per side on the grill, 4½ minutes per side in a skillet.

Meanwhile, make the fried tomato: In a small bowl, mix the rosemary and bread crumbs. Dip the tomato slices in the mixture and coat well on both sides. In a medium sauté pan over medium heat, warm the olive oil and fry the tomatoes until both sides are golden brown, about 4 minutes on each side. Set aside on paper towels.

Make the frico: Preheat the broiler and set the rack 3 to 4 inches away from the heat source. Spray vegetable oil into 8 recessed holders of a cupcake pan and place about ¼ inch of grated Parmigiano-Reggiano in each recess; top with a pinch of chopped parsley and stir to blend using your finger. Place the pan under the broiler and watch closely to avoid burning. When the cheese

for the frico and serving

Vegetable oil spray, such as Pam

Freshly and finely grated Parmigiano-Reggiano, manchego, or Montasio cheese

¼ **cup chopped parsley**

2 **round burger-sized hard rolls, sliced and toasted**

starts to bubble, after about 2 minutes, remove and set aside to cool. Unmold the fricos with a fork and place 2 on each fried tomato slice.

Top 4 roll halves with burgers, fried tomatoes, and frico. Serve open-faced, with a knife and fork.

beer burger smeared with fresh goat cheese

Beer has been brewed and used in marinades for hundreds of years. And today's micro-brews have a great variety of flavors that can heartily flavor meat. For this recipe, I prefer to use a lager for its tangy taste, though most any good beer will do.

serves 4

1 **to 2 tablespoons olive oil (to season grill or skillet)**

2 **pounds lean ground beef sirloin**

¼ **cup lager, at room temperature**

2 **teaspoons honey mustard**

2 **teaspoons fennel seed**

1 **teaspoon finely chopped fresh sage**

½ **teaspoon kosher salt**

½ **teaspoon freshly ground black pepper**

8 **ounces soft goat cheese, such as fresh chèvre, at room temperature**

4 **soft bagels, halved and toasted**

Preheat a grill or cast-iron skillet, wiping down the grate or the skillet with olive oil before heating over a medium-high flame.

In a large bowl, break up the ground beef and pour the beer over it. Let the mixture rest at room temperature for 15 minutes. Mix in the honey mustard, fennel, sage, salt, and pepper. Cover with plastic wrap and refrigerate for 10 minutes.

Divide into 4 patties at least 1 inch thick. Cook the burgers over medium-high heat until medium-rare: 4 minutes per side on the grill, 4½ minutes per side in a skillet.

Meanwhile, smear about 1 tablespoon of goat cheese on the top half of each bagel. Place the burgers on the bottom half of each bagel, cover with the tops, and serve.

dean fearing's mansion roadhouse burger

The famous Mansion on Turtle Creek in Dallas is often referred to as the birthplace of innovative Southwestern cuisine, thanks to the tireless efforts of chef Dean Fearing, whose signature dishes—like his lobster taco and tortilla soup—are admired and imitated far and wide. Feast on this distinctive double cheeseburger and find out how Chef Fearing earned the distinction of being named one of America's Best New Chefs by *Food & Wine*.

serves 4

- 1 to 2 tablespoons olive oil (to season grill or skillet)
- 2 pounds ground beef chuck
- 1 teaspoon kosher salt
- ½ teaspoon freshly ground black pepper
- 8 slices American cheese
- 4 Dean Fearing's Burger Buns (page 92), halved
- 2 tablespoons unsalted butter, melted
- 2 tablespoons mayonnaise
- 2 tablespoons yellow mustard
- 8 iceberg lettuce leaves, washed and dried
- 4 ½-inch-thick slices ripe tomato
- 4 ½-inch-thick slices yellow onion
- 16 dill pickle chips
  Dean Fearing's Tobacco Onion Rings (page 93)
  Ketchup, for serving

Wipe down a grill or a well-seasoned flat griddle with the olive oil, or use a large nonstick sauté pan and preheat over a medium-high flame.

Gently form the ground beef into eight 4-ounce burgers, each about ½ inch thick. Season with the salt and pepper. Cook the burgers over medium-high heat until medium-rare: 4 minutes per side on the grill, 4½ minutes per side in a skillet (see Note). Place 1 slice of the American cheese on each burger to melt, about 1 minute.

Meanwhile, toast the burger buns, butter them generously, and smear each of them with about ½ tablespoon of mayonnaise and mustard.

To serve, place 2 of the burgers, one on top of the other, on the bottom half of each bun. Top each stack of 2 burgers with 2 of the lettuce leaves, a slice each of tomato and onion, and 4 of the pickle chips. Top with the other half of the bun, and serve at once with Tobacco Onion Rings and ketchup.

note: This cooking time will yield a medium-rare burger. For rare, cook 3½ minutes on each side; for medium, cook about 4½ minutes on each side.

stuffed chèvre and caramelized onion burger

Stuffed burgers are a great way to include more flavors and condiments without having to worry that a stacked-up burger won't hold together. I love this stuffing of onions and cheese, but once you get the knack, experiment with your own combinations.

serves 4

1 **tablespoon olive oil, plus 1 to 2 tablespoons to season grill or skillet**

2 **small white onions, finely chopped**

2 **tablespoons Worcestershire sauce**

3 **ounces soft chèvre, or other soft goat's-milk cheese**

2 **pounds ground beef chuck**

2 **teaspoons lightly toasted fennel seeds (see Note, page 69)**

2 **teaspoons powdered ginger**

2 **teaspoons fresh thyme**

½ **teaspoon chili powder**

3 **tablespoons soy sauce**

2 **tablespoons oyster sauce**

4 **onion rolls, sliced and toasted**

Preheat a grill or cast-iron skillet, wiping down the grate or the skillet with 1 or 2 tablespoons olive oil before heating over a medium-high flame.

In a medium saucepan, heat the remaining 1 tablespoon olive oil over a medium flame. Add the onions and cook until softened, then add the Worcestershire sauce and cook, stirring often, until the onions are caramelized, 5 to 10 minutes. Remove from the heat and add the chèvre, stirring to form a paste. Set aside.

In a large bowl, combine the ground chuck, fennel, ginger, thyme, chili powder, soy sauce, and oyster sauce. Mix well using your hands and form into 8 patties. Create small craters in the centers of 4 patties, leaving an edge of about ¼ inch. Place 2 tablespoons of the onion-cheese mixture in the craters. Top with the remaining patties, pinching the seams together. Make sure the stuffing is completely covered.

Cook the burgers over medium-high heat until medium-rare: 4 minutes per side on the grill, 4½ minutes per side in a skillet. Turn the burgers gently to avoid breaking them open. A few minutes before they're finished, add a smear of the leftover goat cheese filling to the top of each burger. Serve on toasted onion rolls.

prosciutto tube brie burger

This easy burger deviates from the norm by its topping of several small prosciutto "tubes"—slices rolled up around a small wedge of cheese. These tubes are placed atop the burgers as they finish cooking, so the cheese melts and the prosciutto's flavor intensifies. I use Brie here, but any easily melted cheese will do.

serves 4

- 1 to 2 tablespoons olive oil (to season grill or skillet)
- 1 pound ground beef chuck
- 1 pound ground veal
- 2 teaspoons minced fresh sage
- ½ pound good prosciutto
- 4 ounces Brie
- 4 sourdough rolls, sliced and toasted
- ½ honeydew melon, seeded and cut into 4 equal wedges, optional

Preheat a grill or cast-iron skillet, wiping down the grate or the skillet with olive oil before heating over a medium-high flame.

In a bowl, combine the ground beef, veal, and sage. Mix well and divide into 4 patties at least 1 inch thick. Cook the burgers over medium-high heat until medium-rare: 4 minutes per side on the grill, 4½ minutes per side in a skillet.

Meanwhile, prepare the prosciutto tubes: Lay slices of prosciutto on a work surface and cut in half (length-wise) so that the pieces are about 3 inches long. Cut off a piece of Brie just large enough to fit across a halved piece of prosciutto, about ¼ inch thick, and place at the end of a prosciutto piece. (Each burger will use about 1 ounce of Brie divided among 5 tubes.) Loosely roll up the Brie in the prosciutto to create a small tube. You should have about 5 mini-tubes per burger, or 20 total.

After flipping the burgers, place 4 or 5 prosciutto tubes on top of each burger and cook, covered, until the cheese melts. When the burgers are done, serve them on toasted rolls with wedges of honeydew on the side, if desired.

lamb, buffalo, venison, & other game burgers

This chapter includes such heavy hitters as David Waltuck's Venison Burger au Poivre and Suzanne Goin's Grilled Lamb Burger with Cumin Yogurt—exciting red-meat alternatives to the traditional beef burger.

delmarva bisonburger

My husband and I created this recipe together, marrying two of our favorite flavors: buffalo meat, a slightly sweet red meat that is low in fat and high in iron, and Old Bay Seasoning, the classic Maryland spice sold in a yellow and blue metal can. I grew up on this spice—in fact, my baby bottles were probably spiked with it. The name Delmarva comes from combining the states Delaware, Maryland, and Virginia, and refers to a peninsula shared by those states, between the Atlantic Ocean and Chesapeake Bay.

serves 4

1 tablespoon olive oil, plus 1 to 2 tablespoons to season grill or skillet

1 large white onion, finely chopped

2 tablespoons beer

1½ tablespoons Old Bay Seasoning (available in most grocery stores)

¼ teaspoon coarsely ground black pepper

2 pounds ground bison

4 slices sharp Cheddar cheese, optional

4 English muffins, split and toasted

Homemade Horseradish Tartar Sauce (see Note), optional

Preheat a grill or cast-iron skillet, wiping down the grate or the skillet with olive oil before heating over a medium-high flame.

In a separate large skillet over medium heat, cook the onion in 1 tablespoon of olive oil until golden brown, about 5 minutes. Pour the beer into the skillet, add the Old Bay Seasoning and pepper, and cook and stir until well blended. Let cool slightly.

In a large bowl, work the onion mixture into the ground bison with your hands. Divide into 4 patties at least ½ inch thick. Cook the burgers over medium-high heat until medium-rare: 3½ minutes per side on the grill, 4 minutes per side in a skillet. For cheeseburgers: 2 minutes before the burgers are finished, top with a slice of Cheddar and cover. Serve on toasted English muffins, smeared with Horseradish Tartar Sauce, if using.

note: To make Horseradish Tartar Sauce: Combine equal parts of spicy whole-grain mustard, prepared or freshly grated horseradish, and prepared tartar sauce.

wanda tornabene's flat veal-and-pork meatball burger

Since 1978, Wanda Tornabene and her daughter, Giovanna, have operated Gangivecchio, a fourteenth-century abbey turned world-class restaurant and inn in Sicily. This recipe converts Wanda's meatball recipe from their first cookbook, *La Cucina Siciliana di Gangivecchio,* into a highly satisfying burger. Serve it between two thick slices of toasted country bread.

serves 4

1	**pound ground veal**
1½	**pounds ground pork**
1	**large egg, lightly beaten**
⅓	**cup freshly chopped parsley**
⅓	**cup freshly grated pecorino**
¾	**cup day-old bread, soaked in water and squeezed dry**
½	**cup diced mortadella or ½ cup diced bologna and ⅛ teaspoon fresh minced garlic**
⅓	**cup diced ham**
½	**cup olive oil**
8	**thick slices fresh country bread, lightly toasted**

In a large bowl, mix together the veal, pork, egg, parsley, pecorino, soaked bread, mortadella, and ham. Divide into 4 equal portions and shape into large balls. Flatten the balls slightly into ovals about 1½ inches thick.

Cover the bottom of a large frying pan with the olive oil and fry the burgers over medium heat until well browned on each side, about 5 minutes.

Serve between slices of the toasted bread.

note: The best method for cooking this delicate burger is in a pan, rather than on a grill. Flip just once to prevent it from falling apart.

suzanne goin's grilled lamb burger with cumin yogurt

Suzanne Goin and Caroline Styne's first restaurant, Lucques (named for Goin's favorite French olive), is a jewel among West Hollywood restaurants on Melrose Avenue. Noted for being "deeply civilized—the experience is about more than just food" (the *Los Angeles Times*), the food is seasonally and devoutly market-driven, never silly or flashy for its own sake. This lamb burger is as unusual as it is succulent. Ask your butcher to grind leg of lamb for you, or do what they do at the restaurant: Chop it finely by hand.

serves 8

- 8 shallots, finely minced
- 3 teaspoons plus 1 tablespoon extra-virgin olive oil
- 1½ teaspoons dried oregano
- 1 teaspoon dried thyme
- 1½ pounds ground or finely chopped lamb
- 1 teaspoon sweet paprika
- ¼ to ½ teaspoon cayenne pepper, to taste
- 1½ tablespoons fennel seeds, toasted (see Note, page 69), and ground with a mortar and pestle or in a spice grinder
- 1½ tablespoons coriander seeds, toasted (see Note, page 69), and ground with a mortar and pestle or in a spice grinder

- 2½ teaspoons kosher salt
- ½ teaspoon plus a pinch freshly ground black pepper
- 3 tablespoons chopped parsley
- 1 cup good-quality whole-milk yogurt (search out yogurt with no pectin or gumlike additives)
- ½ teaspoon cumin seed toasted (see Note, page 69), and ground with a mortar and pestle or in a spice grinder
- 4 sourdough hamburger buns, split and toasted

In a small skillet, cook the shallots gently in 3 teaspoons of the olive oil over medium heat for about 5 minutes. When they are translucent and just starting to color, stir in the oregano and thyme. Remove from the heat and set aside.

In a mixing bowl, combine the lamb, paprika, cayenne, fennel, coriander, 2¼ teaspoons of the salt, the pepper, and parsley. Add the cooked shallots. Make a very small test patty and cook it in a pan. Taste for seasoning and adjust accordingly. Shape the meat into 8 patties.

Make the cumin yogurt: In a mixing bowl, stir the yogurt together with the remaining ¼ teaspoon salt, a pinch of black pepper, and the toasted cumin. Set aside.

When you are ready to grill the burgers, light your grill and wait until the coals are burning red embers, or heat a cast-iron skillet over a medium-high flame. Brush the burgers with the remaining tablespoon of olive oil and cook them just until medium-rare, about 4 minutes per side.

Serve on toasted sourdough buns (very California!), topped with a generous quantity of cumin yogurt.

pita stuffed lamb burger
with sautéed spinach and feta

My daughter's best friend's mother is Greek, and this recipe borrows from the traditional Greek recipes for spanakopita and grilled lamb gyro. The presentation can be elaborate or simply stuffed in a pita pouch, depending on how you feel.

serves 4

for the sautéed spinach

- **1 tablespoon unsalted butter**
- **1 10-ounce package frozen spinach, thawed and squeezed dry**
- **1 teaspoon fennel seeds**
- **1 teaspoon minced garlic**
- **1 teaspoon fresh Greek oregano, chopped, or ½ teaspoon dried**
- **1 cup crumbled Greek feta cheese**
- **2 tablespoons cottage cheese**

for the burger

- **1 to 2 tablespoons olive oil (to season grill or skillet)**
- **2 pounds ground lamb**
- **1 teaspoon minced garlic**
- **1 tablespoon chopped parsley**
- **1 teaspoon sweet paprika**
- **1 teaspoon freshly ground black pepper**
- **1 lemon, halved, plus 2 sliced lemons, for garnish**
- **4 large pita pockets**

Preheat a grill or cast-iron skillet, wiping down the grate or the skillet with olive oil before heating over a medium-high flame.

Make the sautéed spinach: In a medium saucepan, melt the butter over medium heat. Add the spinach, fennel, garlic, and oregano. Stirring constantly, cook until the liquid evaporates, about 4 minutes. Add the feta and cottage cheese and stir until creamy, about 4 minutes. Keep warm over very low heat.

Make the burgers: In a large bowl, combine the lamb and the garlic, parsley, paprika, and pepper. Mix well and divide into 4 patties at least ¾ inch thick. Cook the burgers over medium-high heat until medium-rare: 4 to 4½ minutes per side on the grill or in a skillet. A few minutes before removing, squeeze both lemon halves over the burgers.

Slice open one end of each pita, spoon the spinach mixture atop the burgers, then tuck them into the pita, and serve with lemon slices for garnish. This burger can be eaten with a fork and knife or with your hands.

spicy buffalo burger with pepper monterey jack

This recipe is quite a crowd pleaser: It is simple, spicy, slightly sweet, and very cheesy—great qualities in any burger. My younger brother, a spice enthusiast, doubles my suggested Tabasco amount. If you follow his lead, make sure to serve this burger with a tall, cold glass of water.

serves 4

for the burgers

- 1 **to 2 tablespoons olive oil (to season grill or skillet)**
- 6 **shakes of Tabasco sauce for mildly spicy (double it for extra-spicy)**
- 2 **tablespoons Worcestershire sauce**
- 2 **tablespoons chopped cilantro**
- ¼ **teaspoon kosher salt**

  A few grinds of black pepper
- 2 **tablespoons finely chopped white onion**
- 2 **pounds ground buffalo**
- 8 **slices pepper Monterey Jack**
- 4 **fresh kaiser rolls, sliced and toasted**

Preheat grill or cast-iron skillet, wiping down the grate or the skillet with olive oil before heating over a medium-high flame.

In a large bowl, combine the Tabasco and Worcestershire sauces, cilantro, salt, pepper, and onion. Taste carefully to test the spice level. Keep in mind that once it's folded in the meat and cooked it will be about half as spicy. Add extra Tabasco if you like your food super-spicy.

Divide into 4 patties at least ½ inch thick. Cook the burgers over medium-high heat until medium-rare: 3½ minutes per side on the grill, 4 minutes per side in a skillet. Cook for no more than 4 minutes per side—do not overcook! About 2 minutes before removing from the heat, place 2 cheese slices on each burger to melt. Serve on toasted rolls with plenty of water nearby.

david waltuck's venison burger au poivre

At the incomparable Chanterelle in Manhattan, David Waltuck's tremendous skill and unflagging originality have earned him an exalted place in the pantheon of great American chefs. Waltuck opened the original Chanterelle with his wife Karen when both were in their early twenties, in a then-remote area of SoHo. Karen quickly became the most cordial and soothing hostess in town. It wasn't long before the restaurant's international reputation and tremendous popularity necessitated larger quarters, and Chanterelle moved to commodious TriBeCa. In July 2000, David and Karen opened a second TriBeCa restaurant, Le Zinc, a casual brasserie. Waltuck's style mingles classic French techniques with unlimited imagination, and this bunless venison burger au poivre, which he created especially for this book, is that qualitative blend made manifest. Venison has practically no fat, and because, as Waltuck is fond of saying, "fat equals flavor," you should have your butcher grind in 4 ounces of beef fat with the 2 pounds of venison. The fat will also keep the venison burger from becoming too dry. Serve with mashed potatoes or fries.

serves 4

2 pounds venison hamburger meat (ground venison with 4 ounces beef fat ground in)

¼ cup all-purpose flour

1 teaspoon kosher salt

3 tablespoons canola or other neutral oil

3 tablespoons brandy

¼ cup medium-dry Madeira, or French dry white vermouth

1 tablespoon coarsely cracked black pepper, plus more to taste

1 teaspoon coarsely ground pink peppercorns

1 teaspoon coarsely ground Szechuan peppercorns

1 pint heavy cream

1 tablespoon veal glaze (veal stock reduced to syrupy consistency, available at gourmet food shops), optional

Juice of ½ lemon

Gently form the ground venison into 4 thick 8-ounce patties. Do not overwork or knead the meat. Lightly flour and season with the salt.

Heat a sauté pan over high flame, add the oil, then the burgers. Promptly turn the heat down to medium and cook 3 to 4 minutes on each side for rare; do not cook venison beyond medium-rare or it will dry out. Remove the burgers from the pan and set aside on a warm plate.

While cooking the burgers, make the sauce in a clean pan. Off heat, add the brandy and Madeira. Put the pan over medium heat and reduce the liquid until almost dry, about 15 minutes. Add the peppers, cream, veal glaze (if using), and lemon juice. Reduce over high heat until thickened, about 5 minutes. Taste and season with salt and more pepper if needed.

Put the burgers on plates (don't serve on a bun) and pour the hot pepper sauce over them.

note: The sauce may be started first—just avoid letting it sit out too long (more than 5 minutes) or a skin will develop on its surface. A few minutes after you begin the sauce, start cooking the burger.

claude troisgros's foie gras burger

Chef Claude Troisgros, owner of the restaurant Claude Troisgros in Rio de Janeiro, Brazil, and consulting chef at the celebrity-packed Blue Door Restaurant in Miami, has three generations of cooking in his blood. Influenced by his grandfather Jean-Baptiste, close friend and fellow chef Paul Bocuse, and the natural ingredients of Brazil, his illustrious signature French-Brazilian fusion style was born. Chef Claude once had the pleasure of creating this burger for former president Bill Clinton. Tuck into this new Troisgros twist on foie gras and get in touch with your presidential appetite.

serves 4

for the caramelized onions

- 1 tablespoon olive oil
- 2 red onions, thinly sliced
- 1 tablespoon (packed) dark brown sugar
- 2 tablespoons soy sauce
  Salt and freshly ground black pepper to taste

for the sauce

- 1/2 yellow onion, peeled and sliced
- 2 teaspoons olive oil
- 2 garlic cloves, peeled and minced
- 8 medium beefsteak tomatoes, peeled, seeded, and chopped
- 1 tablespoon balsamic vinegar
- 1 tablespoon tomato paste
- 1 tablespoon honey
  Tabasco sauce to taste
  Salt to taste

for the foie gras and serving

- 4 pieces of foie gras, Grade A, sliced 1/4 inch thick and scored
- 1/2 teaspoon kosher salt
  Freshly ground black pepper
- 4 hamburger buns
- 1/2 cup baby greens, lightly seasoned with salt, pepper, and olive oil
  Olive oil

Make the caramelized onions: In a large sauté pan, heat the olive oil over a medium flame until it slides easily across the pan. Add the sliced red onions and cook until brown and soft, 10 to 15 minutes. Add the brown sugar and let the onions caramelize, stirring gently for about 5 minutes. Add the soy sauce, season lightly with salt and pepper, and set aside.

Make the sauce: In a skillet over medium heat, gently cook the yellow onion in 2 teaspoons of olive oil with the garlic. Add the tomatoes and stir. Stir in the balsamic vinegar, tomato paste, and honey and let the mixture simmer for 5 minutes. Remove from the heat and purée in a blender until it looks like ketchup. Season with the Tabasco and salt, and set aside.

Sear the foie gras: Turn on all the ventilation in the kitchen—fois gras can create a lot of smoke. Place the scored foie gras on a plate and season with 2 pinches of kosher salt and 1 grind of black pepper. Place the slices in a preheated, clean, dry sauté pan and sear for 30 seconds on each side. Remove and drain on paper towels.

Place a large spoonful of tomato sauce in the middle of each of 4 plates and spread it around. Slice and toast the buns. Place the bottom halves of the bun on the sauce and cover with the caramelized onions, then a piece of foie gras for each. Place the seasoned baby greens on the foie gras and top with the other bun halves. Lightly drizzle olive oil on the plate around your burgers and eat with a knife and fork. Leftover tomato sauce will keep, refrigerated, for up to 1 week.

chicken, turkey, fish, seafood, and vegetarian burgers

When you long for something different, this chapter is the place to turn. Here you'll find a tuna burger recipe inspired by the fabled Union Square Café, and a most unusual Tofu-Encrusted Coconut Burger with Pineapple Almond Slices—so delightful that it might well tempt you to go vegetarian (at least for one meal).

patricia yeo's thai-style chicken burger with spicy peanut "ketchup" and asian slaw

A former sous chef for Bobby Flay at his Mesa Grill and Bolo restaurants in Manhattan, Patricia Yeo broke out on her own at AZ and then Pazo, while also writing *Cooking from A to Z.* Yeo's culinary style bridges the best of American and Asian cuisine and is as good as fusion gets. This recipe, created especially for *Burgers,* blends ground chicken with fresh ingredients for an easy, healthy, and flavorful meal. The "ketchup" and colorful Asian slaw are well worth the effort.

serves 4

for the burgers

- 3 **pounds ground chicken, preferably thigh meat**
- 1 **onion, very finely minced**
- 2 **stalks lemongrass, white and light green parts only, very finely minced**
- 2 **tablespoons freshly grated turmeric, or 2 teaspoons turmeric powder**
- 2 **tablespoons freshly grated galangal, or ginger root, optional**
- ¼ **cup finely diced jalapeños, stemmed and seeded**
- 2 **garlic cloves, finely minced**
- ¼ **cup finely chopped cilantro**
- 2 **tablespoons fish sauce (optional)**
- 1 **egg white**

Salt and freshly ground black pepper to taste

- 4 **brioche buns**

Spicy Peanut "Ketchup" (recipe follows)

Asian Slaw (recipe follows)

Preheat the grill to high.

In a large bowl, mix together all the ingredients using your hands, making sure that everything is distributed evenly. Divide the mixture evenly into 4 large balls, and roll each ball between your palms to make sure there are no seams. Flatten the balls into ¾-inch-thick patties. Grill over high heat for approximately 7 minutes per side, until the burgers have a nice char. Serve in brioche buns smeared with the Spicy Peanut "Ketchup" with Asian Slaw on the side.

spicy peanut "ketchup"

½ cup sliced shallots

2 garlic cloves, finely minced

¼ cup canola oil

4 jalapeño peppers, stemmed, seeded, and finely chopped

½ cup oil-packed sun-dried tomatoes, cut into strips

3 roasted red bell peppers, peeled, stemmed, and seeded

¼ cup red wine

¼ cup smooth peanut butter

Sherry vinegar

Salt and freshly ground black pepper

In a large sauté pan over medium-low heat, cook the shallots and garlic in the canola oil until translucent, approximately 10 minutes. Add the jalapeños, sun-dried tomatoes, and red peppers. Cook over high heat for 5 more minutes, then add the red wine. Lower the heat and simmer, stirring occasionally, until the wine has boiled away, approximately 10 to 15 minutes.

Remove from the heat, let cool, then purée in a blender. Fold in the peanut butter. Season to taste with vinegar, salt, and pepper. If the mixture seems a little too thick, stir in a little more red wine or water.

asian slaw

½ cup Japanese pickled ginger, drained and finely chopped

2 tablespoons rice wine vinegar

1 teaspoon sugar

1 cup mayonnaise

1 medium cucumber, peeled, seeded, and cut into 2-inch matchsticks (about 1 cup)

1 cup julienned Napa cabbage leaves

2 medium carrots, peeled and cut into 2-inch matchsticks (about 1 cup)

1 large red bell pepper, stemmed, seeded, and cut into 1-inch matchsticks (about 1 cup)

In a medium bowl, stir the ginger, vinegar, and sugar into the mayonnaise. At least 1 hour before serving (but not more than 3 hours), toss the remaining ingredients with the mayonnaise mixture. Refrigerate until ready to serve.

bbq chicken burger

I recommend that you prepare this recipe with both white and dark ground chicken meat—the burger will be juicer and more flavorful. However, if you are watching your weight, use only skinless chicken breast, and enjoy a mere 2 grams of fat and a little over 200 calories per serving. When I visit my amazingly fit, health-conscious family—my parents in small-town Pennsylvania or my soap opera–star sister in Hollywood—that is the version I rely on when summoned to the stove.

serves 4

- 1 **to 2 tablespoons olive oil (to season grill or skillet)**
- ½ **pound ground chicken breast (see Note)**
- 1 **pound ground chicken thighs (see Note)**
- 3 **tablespoons finely minced fresh parsley**
- ¼ **roasted red pepper in oil, diced**
- ½ **teaspoon kosher salt**
- 1 **cup prepared barbecue sauce**
- 4 **slices sharp Cheddar cheese, optional**
- 1 **green bell pepper, sliced into rings about ¼ inch thick (about 8 rings), top, bottom, and seeds discarded**
- 1 **yellow bell pepper, sliced into rings about ¼ inch thick (about 8 rings), top, bottom, and seeds discarded**
- 8 **large slices pumpernickel bread, toasted**

Preheat a grill or cast-iron skillet, wiping down the grate or the skillet with olive oil before heating over a medium flame.

Place the ground chicken in a medium bowl and season with the parsley, roasted red pepper, and salt. Mix together using your hands and form 4 patties about ¾ inch thick. Place the burgers on a plate and coat them generously with barbecue sauce, about ¼ cup.

Cook the burgers over medium heat until the center of the burgers is opaque: 5 minutes per side on the grill, 7 minutes per side in a skillet. While grilling, continuously coat the burgers with any remaining BBQ sauce. For cheeseburgers, 4 minutes before the patties are finished, top with the cheese and cover to melt.

Meanwhile, grill the bell pepper slices for about 2 minutes per side and set aside, until the burgers are done.

Serve between the slices of toasted bread with a few slices of grilled green and yellow bell peppers.

note: To make ground chicken, cut 1½ pounds of skinless chicken meat into ½-inch cubes. Place in a food processor and pulse just enough to hold a patty shape (about 30 seconds).

oat-molasses turkey burger
with vermont cheddar

My older sister lives in Vermont, where she turned me on to the simple yet uncommon uses of farm-fresh ingredients. These infused favors will have you feeling the wonderful comfort of breakfast any time of the day.

serves 4

1   to 2 tablespoons olive oil (to season grill or skillet)
4   tablespoons quick-cooking oatmeal
4   tablespoons Vermont maple syrup
4   teaspoons molasses
2   pounds ground turkey
8   ¾-ounce slices Vermont Cheddar
4   large soft flour wraps

Preheat a grill or cast-iron skillet, wiping down the grate or the skillet with olive oil before heating over a medium-high flame.

In a small bowl, combine the oatmeal, maple syrup, and molasses. Set aside until the oats are softened, about 10 minutes. Transfer to a large bowl and mix well with the ground turkey. Form into 4 oblong burgers about ¾ inch thick (this shape will roll more efficiently in the wraps).

Cook the burgers until done through: 5 minutes per side on the grill, and 7 minutes per side in a skillet. A few minutes before removing the burgers, place 2 slices of Cheddar on each and cover the grill or skillet to melt the cheese. Serve each burger rolled up in a wrap, sliced in half.

cafeteria's turkey burger
with citrus vinaigrette salad

Cafeteria currently caters to fashionable crowds in Miami and Manhattan, and is poised to open its third 24/7 stylish comfort-food restaurant in tony NoHo. Cafeteria created this turkey burger to offer succor to frenzied denizens of the night—without compromising those all-important waistlines. Serve with Cafeteria's Baked Fries (page 77).

serves 4

1 to 2 tablespoons olive oil (to season grill), or 1 tablespoon peanut oil (to season skillet)

2 pounds ground turkey

¼ cup prepared horseradish

¼ cup chopped flat-leaf parsley

1 tablespoon plus 1 pinch kosher salt

1 teaspoon plus 1 pinch freshly ground black pepper

⅛ cup fresh orange juice (from about ½ orange)

2 teaspoons fresh lime juice (from less than ½ lime)

⅛ cup blended oil (see Note)

1 teaspoon balsamic vinegar

1½ ounces mesclun greens

4 Pepperidge Farms buns

4 half-sour pickle halves

4 ½-inch slices red tomatoes

4 ¼-inch slices red onion

2 whole Hass avocados, peeled, pitted, and sliced

Preheat a grill or skillet to medium-high, wiping down the grill grate with olive oil or the skillet with peanut oil before heating over a medium-high flame.

In a large bowl, combine the turkey, horseradish, parsley, 1 tablespoon salt, and 1 teaspoon pepper. Mix well and form into four 8-ounce patties.

Cook the burgers until cooked through: 5 minutes per side on the grill, and 7 minutes per side in a skillet.

In another bowl, whisk together the orange and lime juices with the blended oil, vinegar, and the remaining pinches of salt and pepper. Drizzle 1 tablespoon of the mixture onto the greens and store the leftovers in the refrigerator for up to 1 week.

Place the burgers between the buns and garnish with pickles, tomatoes, onion, and avocado. Serve with the dressed mesclun greens.

note: Blended oils such as canola oil and olive oil are becoming more popular and can be found in your grocery store. Canola is low in fat, yet it has no distinct flavor, whereas olive oil is twice as high in fat, but has a pleasing taste. By combining the two oils, you get a lower-fat, more flavorful product—the best of both worlds.

chesapeake crab cake burger

When I was growing up, every summer weekend, my father's family would pull out the newspapers, line the picnic tables, and have a crab feast overlooking the Chesapeake Bay. It was during one of those festive occasions that I had my first crab cake. My grandmother, Edna, had a secret to her crab cakes: Simply put, "Don't mix it up too much"— wise advice that I use to this day.

serves 4

- 1 **large egg, beaten**
- 3 **tablespoons mayonnaise**
- 2 **tablespoons finely chopped pimientos**
- 8 **crumbled no-salt saltine crackers (4 to go inside crab cake, 4 to coat crab cake)**
- 1 **teaspoon kosher salt**
- 2 **teaspoons Old Bay Seasoning (for mild flavor; add 2 extra teaspoons for a spicier version)**
- 2 **tablespoons finely chopped parsley**
- 1 **pound lump crabmeat, picked over for shell slivers and cartilage**
- ¼ **cup vegetable oil, for frying**
- 4 **white rolls, sliced and toasted**
- 4 **¼-inch-thick tomato slices, optional**
- ¾ **cup prepared tartar sauce, for serving**

In a medium bowl, combine the egg, mayonnaise, pimiento, 4 of the crumbled crackers, salt, Old Bay, and parsley. Mix well. Gently fold in the crabmeat and form into 4 patties without "mixing it up too much." The patties will be fairly wet. Gently coat with the remaining 4 crumbled crackers on both sides.

Preheat a skillet, coat the bottom with the vegetable oil, and fry the crab cakes over medium-high heat until golden brown, about 2 minutes per side. Gently turn with a thin metal spatula.

Place a crab cake on each roll with a tomato slice, if using, and serve with a ramekin of tartar sauce for dipping.

cooking crab cakes

The trick here is to fry the crab cake quickly before it falls apart. More expensive crabmeat, mostly "back fin," is sometimes so lumpy that it doesn't hold together. In that case, I break apart a few of the lumps so there will be smaller pieces to help hold it together. Another trick is to include more mayo, but I would do that only as a last resort.

norman van aken's tuna burger with mojo

Last year, while my family was down in sunny Key West, my husband and I were summoned to a dinner meeting two hours away in Coral Gables. The meeting was held at Norman's, one of Florida's most popular restaurants. Chowing down on Chef Norman's signature blend of Latin, Caribbean, Asian, and American flavors, I was awed by the healthy yet vibrant fare, such as this burger.

serves 4

20 ounces fresh tuna, cut into ½-inch cubes

¼ cup Norman's Mojo (recipe follows)

¼ cup olive oil

4 fresh hamburger buns, split and toasted

In a food processor, briefly pulse the tuna cubes 3 or 4 times, just enough that the pieces can hold a patty shape. Move the mixture to a bowl and thoroughly blend in the prepared mojo with your hands. Make four 5-ounce patties and chill, covered, for 2 hours.

Heat the olive oil in a large skillet over a medium-high flame and sear the tuna burgers until browned outside and medium-rare, about 2 to 3 minutes per side. Serve on the toasted buns.

norman's mojo

makes 1½ cups

6 garlic cloves, minced

1 Scotch bonnet chile, stemmed,
   seeded, and minced (wear rubber
   gloves if your skin is sensitive to
   hot peppers)

2 teaspoons freshly toasted cumin
   seeds (see Note)

½ teaspoon kosher salt

1 cup olive oil

⅓ cup fresh sour orange juice (or
   equal parts lime and orange
   juices)

2 teaspoons Spanish sherry vinegar
   Freshly ground black pepper to
   taste

With a mortar and pestle, mash together the garlic, chile, cumin, and salt until fairly smooth.

Heat the olive oil in a skillet over a medium flame. When nearly smoking, carefully add the garlic-chile mixture and stir well. Remove from the heat and set the mixture aside for 10 minutes, then whisk in the orange juice and vinegar and season with pepper to taste.

Leftover mojo can be reserved for other uses and stored in the refrigerator for up to 1 week. Try it as a marinade for chicken or flank steaks.

note: Toasting whole seeds, spices, and nuts intensifies their flavor, and in the case of nuts and seeds it also imparts crunchiness. For this recipe, place the cumin seeds in a small, dry sauté pan over medium heat and cook for about 5 minutes, stirring constantly. This method also works with toasting other spices and nuts.

john jr.'s grilled vegetable burger

Even the most devout carnivores need to switch gears. This burger is best in spring and summer when local fresh vegetables and herbs are available and you can grill outside. My older brother, John Jr., created this burger partly to teach me a thing or two about cooking, but mostly to remind me that he still craves friendly competition.

serves 4

1 to 2 tablespoons olive oil (to season grill)

4 portobello mushrooms, stems removed

½ fennel bulb, fronds removed, peeled, and sliced ⅜ inch thick

1 yellow bell pepper, stemmed, seeded, and quartered

1 small Bermuda onion, sliced lengthwise and layers pulled apart

1 large zucchini, sliced ⅜ inch thick

1 large yellow squash, sliced ⅜ inch thick

8 ounces cream cheese (or nonfat cream cheese)

2 cups shredded manchego (or nonfat cheese)

4 stalks rosemary, leaves removed and minced, stems reserved

2 tablespoons olive oil

2 teaspoons kosher salt

2 teaspoons cracked black pepper

Preheat the oven to 450°F. and preheat a seasoned grill to medium-high. When the grill is hot, put on the portobello and fennel, and grill them for 10 minutes. Add the yellow pepper, onion, zucchini, and squash and continue grilling for another 5 minutes, or until you can easily pass a knife through the vegetables. Remove and set aside.

Soften the cream cheese by microwaving it for 30 seconds or so. Scrape it into a work bowl, add the shredded manchego, and mix until well blended.

Line a cookie sheet with aluminum foil and make 4 stacks of the vegetables, smearing the cheese mixture in between each vegetable. I recommend putting them in the following order (bottom to top): portobello, fennel, yellow pepper, onion, zucchini, and squash.

After making the stacks, pierce each through with a metal skewer, then replace the skewer with a sturdy rosemary stalk (see Note). Drizzle the stacks with olive oil and season with the salt and pepper.

Bake the stacks for 5 minutes, until the cheese has melted. Serve hot on a large plate.

note: Sometimes a rosemary stalk just does not want to go through the veggies. If that's the case, stick it in as far as it will go and also use a short skewer.

yellowfin tuna burger with mandarin orange–ginger glaze

When Union Square Café created their Yellowfin Tuna Burger in the late 1980s, it was the most famous burger in Manhattan—perhaps even in the whole country. I first tried this burger several years ago and then again just last week, and it remains one of my favorites. Restaurateur Danny Meyer and chef Michael Romano credit the late, great chef Pierre Franey for this invention. I've given the burger and its glaze some delicious new twists.

serves 4

for the glaze

- 1 **tablespoon teriyaki sauce**
- 1 **tablespoon soy sauce**
- ½ **teaspoon minced fresh ginger**
- ½ **teaspoon minced garlic**
- 1 **tablespoon honey**
- ⅓ **cup canned Mandarin oranges, drained and chopped, plus 2 tablespoons canning juice**

for the burgers

- 2 **pounds yellowfin tuna**
- 2 **teaspoons minced garlic**
- 3 **tablespoons toasted pecans, pulverized in a spice grinder**
- 1 **teaspoon kosher salt**
- ¼ **teaspoon freshly ground black pepper**
- ¼ **cup sesame oil**
- 4 **fresh burger buns, toasted and buttered**

Make the glaze: Combine all the glaze ingredients with ⅓ cup water in a 1-quart saucepan and bring to a boil. Lower the heat and simmer until the glaze coats the back of a spoon, about 10 minutes. Strain through a sieve and reserve in a warm place until the burgers are cooked. Skip the straining step if you like chunky glazes.

Make the burgers: Remove any skin or gristle from the tuna, then grind in a meat grinder or chop with a clean sharp knife just to the texture of hamburger meat. If you have a food processor, you should chop the tuna into cubes first and use the dough blade to mince.

Transfer the ground tuna to a bowl and combine with the garlic, ground pecans, salt, and pepper. Mix thoroughly. Divide the tuna into 4 equal portions. Using your hands, roll each into a smooth ball and then flatten into a compact patty.

Heat the sesame oil in a large skillet over a medium-high flame and sear the burgers until browned outside and medium-rare, about 2 to 3 minutes per side. Serve each on a buttered, toasted bun topped with 1 tablespoon of the warm glaze.

tofu-encrusted coconut burger with pineapple almond slices

While dining at Disney's Brown Derby on a recent family vacation, amidst the chaos and the hordes of children (mine were throwing pasta at each other), I sampled an amazing dish that got me thinking about how to bring flavorful variety to tofu. This dish honors that meal with my own special version, a temptation to become a vegetarian!

serves 4

- 1 **package extra-firm tofu, about 12 ounces, cut into four 1-inch-thick slices**
- ½ **cup plus 2 tablespoons unsweetened coconut milk**
- ½ **cup all-purpose flour**
- ¼ **cup cornstarch**
- ½ **cup coconut flakes**
- 1½ **cups olive oil, for frying**
- 4 **canned pineapple rings, at room temperature, canning juice reserved**
- ¼ **cup sliced toasted almonds**
- 8 **thin slices 7-grain bread, toasted**

Place 4 tofu slices on a work surface and spread each with a tablespoon of coconut milk. Let it rest for a few minutes, then turn the tofu over and apply a tablespoon of coconut milk to each of the other sides.

In a large bowl, combine the flour, cornstarch, and coconut flakes. Gently coat the marinated tofu with the flour mixture; make sure the tofu is well coated on all sides. Set aside for a few minutes. Reserve the flour mixture.

Pour the olive oil in a medium skillet, and place over medium heat. When the oil is hot, add the tofu. Flip carefully as soon as the coconut flakes turn golden brown, frying about 3 minutes per side. Remove and drain on paper towels.

Meanwhile, in a small sauté pan over medium heat, add the juice from the canned pineapple and stir in the almonds. Add 2 teaspoons of the flour mixture and the remaining 2 tablespoons of coconut milk, lower the heat, and stir until thick, about 5 minutes.

Serve the tofu on toasted bread topped with the pineapple slices and the almond mixture.

sides
and condiments

Even the greatest burgers can benefit from the assistance of sides and condiments. This section provides the basic recipes, from fries to ketchup, with more than a few suggested alternatives and twists.

Mama's Mac-'n'-Cheese

Roy's Maui Onion Salad

Geoffrey Zakarian's Town Gingered Cole Slaw

Sautéed Onions

Autumn Bacon-Apple Potato Salad

José's Avocado Ketchup

Garden Summer Ketchup

Crispy Potato Chips

Winter Ketchup

Cafeteria's Baked Fries

Geoffrey Zakarian's Town Buttered Chips

Dean Fearing's Burger Buns

Dean Fearing's Tobacco Onion Rings

Mayonnaise

Roasted Garlic and Infused Olive Oil

Jonathan Waxman's Fries

crispy potato chips

Store-bought chips can be great, but there's nothing like chowing down on piping hot fresh chips flavored just the way you like them. Store-bought chips may also contain additives and preservatives, whereas these chips are as fresh as they come, and *so* delicious.

serves 4

4 Idaho potatoes
1½ quarts vegetable oil, for frying
  Kosher salt to taste

Rinse the potatoes and slice them about ¹⁄₁₆ inch thick or paper-thin, preferably using a mandoline. Place the potato slices in a large sieve and lower the sieve into a bowl of very cold water. Shake the sieve, then lift from the water. Rinse with cold water until the water runs clear. Dry the potatoes as best you can with either a salad spinner or paper towels. It's important to dry the potatoes thoroughly; water will make the oil splatter.

Pour the oil into a heavy pot or deep fryer. If you're using an electric fryer, follow the manufacturer's instructions for oil quantity. Bring the oil to 320°F., using a deep-frying thermometer for accurate readings (see Deep-Frying Temperatures, right). Fry the potatoes in small batches for about 10 to 15 minutes, or until they are light brown. Continually stir the chips so they cook evenly. When golden, remove the chips and place on paper towels to drain. Sprinkle at once with kosher salt to taste and one of the suggested seasonings (see Variations). Serve while hot.

variations

- **Garlic:** Stir 1 tablespoon of minced garlic into 3 tablespoons of melted butter and pour over the chips.

- **Old Bay:** Stir 2 teaspoons of Old Bay Seasoning into 3 tablespoons of melted butter and pour over the chips.

- **Parsley:** Stir 2 tablespoons of chopped parsley into 3 tablespoons of melted butter and pour over the chips.

deep-frying temperatures

Whenever you're deep-frying without the assistance of a candy or deep-frying thermometer, gauge the oil's temperature by sprinkling some flour into it. If the flour browns almost immediately, the oil is ready to fry chips, fries, or onion rings. I heat the oil over a medium-low flame in a heavy pot. My motto is: Fry slow and low. If you rush the deep-frying process, especially with starches, you may end up with a burnt flavor.

cafeteria's baked fries

These fries are first baked and then fried. This means you can cut the potatoes into wider pieces because they are cooked through before they're fried; the hot oil serves to make their skins crispy.

serves 4

6 large Idaho potatoes, scrubbed

⅛ cup blended oil (see Note, page 65)

1 tablespoon kosher salt, plus more for serving

1 teaspoon cracked black pepper

2 cups vegetable oil

Heat the oven to 350°F. On a baking sheet, toss the whole potatoes with the blended oil, 1 teaspoon of the salt, and the pepper. Roast for 60 minutes. Let cool completely and cut into lengths ⅛ inch thick.

In a deep pot or fryer, heat the vegetable oil to 375°F. Fry the potatoes in batches, for 8 to 10 minutes, or until golden. Toss with additional kosher salt to taste.

geoffrey zakarian's town buttered chips

Clarified butter cooks at a higher temperature than regular butter, without breaking down or smoking, making it a great frying agent. This recipe also calls for canola oil, a relatively flavorless, lowfat oil, which allows the butter's natural flavors to shine through while keeping the fat and calories in check.

serves 4

2 **to 3 medium russet potatoes, washed and sliced paper-thin crosswise on a mandoline**

1 **quart canola oil**

1 **quart clarified butter (see Note)**

1 **teaspoon fine sea salt**

Rinse the sliced potatoes in cold running water for a few minutes to remove excess starch. Drain well, and pat dry; the potatoes must be completely dry. In a large, deep stockpot, heat the oil and clarified butter to 350°F. (see page 77). Lightly fry in small batches until crisp and golden brown, about 15 minutes, making sure to move the potatoes constantly during the frying so that they color evenly. Remove them from the oil to drain on a flat pan lined with paper towels. Season immediately with the sea salt.

note: You can find clarified butter in many large supermarkets under the name *ghee,* typically used in Indian cooking. Ghee is made by melting butter slowly over a low flame and then separating the layers that form: The top layer is a thin layer of foam, which is skimmed off; the middle and largest layer is the clarified butter; and the bottom layer is where the water and most of the milk solids remain. These can be removed through straining and decanting. It's an involved process that makes purchasing ghee more than worthwhile.

mayonnaise

I love homemade mayonnaise and its many variations. The whipping process always seems to take a little longer than I would like, and that's why I recommend using an electric mixer. Homemade mayonnaise will keep for up to 10 days, covered and refrigerated.

yields 1¾ cups

1	**large egg**
½	**teaspoon kosher salt**
½	**teaspoon dry mustard powder**
1	**pinch sugar**
1	**pinch cayenne pepper**
1¼	**cups vegetable oil**
2	**tablespoons white vinegar**
1	**to 2 tablespoons freshly squeezed lemon juice (from about ½ lemon), or to taste**

I recommend using a standing mixer. If you don't have one, an electric hand mixer will do. Otherwise, beat with a whisk, though that will be very labor-intensive.

Place the egg in a bowl and whip at medium speed until well mixed. In a separate bowl, combine the salt, mustard powder, sugar, and cayenne, and beat into the egg until well blended. Turn the mixer on high and add ½ cup of the oil in a slow stream, one drop at a time, until it emulsifies and thickens. Once the mixture emulsifies, you can add the oil more quickly. Add 2 tablespoons of white vinegar and continue whipping. Add in the remaining oil and continue whipping. Taste carefully, adjust the flavor by adding lemon juice or more white vinegar, and beat until the mixture reaches mayonnaise consistency.

variations

- **Horseradish:** Beat in freshly grated or prepared horseradish to taste.

- **Aïoli:** Add the pulp of half a roasted head of garlic (or to taste) to the eggs and proceed as above.

- **Herb Spread:** After making the basic mayonnaise, beat in finely chopped fresh herbs, such as basil, cilantro, or rosemary.

roasted garlic and infused olive oil

I love roasted garlic for its mild but robust taste. For many recipes, I prefer it to raw garlic, which can be overpowering. Roasted garlic has many uses—it's great for blending with softened butter, serving in burgers, or sprucing up vinaigrettes. Once roasted, the garlic may be refrigerated up to 2 weeks.

yields ¾ cup

for the roasted garlic
- **4 large heads of garlic, unpeeled**
- **¼ cup olive oil**

for the infused olive oil
- **1 cup olive oil**
- **1 sprig rosemary**
- **Freshly ground black pepper**

To roast the garlic: Preheat the oven to 350°F.

Remove the outer skin of the garlic head and place the unpeeled cloves in a large piece of aluminum foil. Equally distribute ¼ cup of olive oil amongst the cloves, then wrap tightly in the foil.

Place the garlic in the oven and bake for 30 minutes. When the cloves are done, they should be soft and golden. To eat, gently squeeze a softened clove out of its peel. Store the unpeeled roasted cloves in a plastic container in the refrigerator for up to 2 weeks.

To infuse the oil: Gently squeeze out 6 roasted garlic cloves and place them in a small saucepan. Add the olive oil, rosemary, and a few grinds of black pepper, and cook over low heat for 10 minutes. Stir carefully to avoid breaking up the cloves. Remove from the heat and place in a clean glass container. Use immediately, or refrigerate (for up to 1 week) to discourage the growth of bacteria.

When you want to use the infused oil again, simply heat the solidified oil in a saucepan or microwave until it becomes liquid. Reheating infused olive oil will begin to change the flavor, so I recommend doing this only once.

These famed fries are easy to make and a great side dish.

serves 4 to 6

4 large potatoes (preferably from Klamath Falls, Oregon, or russets)

Peanut, safflower, or corn oil (*not* canola oil), for deep-frying

Peel the potatoes and soak overnight in cold water. The next day, cut the potatoes into thin fries with cross-sections about ¼ inch square and soak them again for another 2 or 3 hours.

Add 2 cups of oil per potato to a deep, heavy pot or fryer. The oil should fill the pot at least one third of the way, or the fryer as the manufacturer's instructions suggest. Heat the oil to 250°F. (see page 77) and cook the fries for 8 minutes. Remove with a slotted spoon, cool on paper towels, and refrigerate for up to 12 hours. Do not discard the oil.

When ready to serve, deep-fry the fries again at 350°F. for 2 or 3 minutes, until golden.

the pros and cons
of soaking potatoes

Pro: Soaking potatoes in cold water helps remove some of the starch and makes them less sticky. However . . .

Con: Soaking potatoes in water may deplete nutrients and flavor.

What to do? Go ahead and soak them—they'll still taste great.

mama's mac-'n'-cheese

This recipe combines two contrasting cheese flavors to create a savory blend: Muenster is mild to mellow and Cheddar is robust and somewhat sharp. However, this recipe is flexible and invites different cheese pairings. If you like piquant flavors, try blue cheese with Muenster; for a buttery, nutty flavor, try Parmigiano-Reggiano. The possibilities are endless. If you're making this for kids, try American cheese and serve it directly from the pot—you can skip the broiling or baking.

serves 4

2 tablespoons olive oil

1½ cups uncooked elbow macaroni

2 tablespoons unsalted butter

¼ cup shredded Muenster cheese

¾ cup shredded Cheddar cheese

½ teaspoon kosher salt

1 pinch freshly ground black pepper

⅓ cup whole milk

1 tablespoon all-purpose flour

1 tablespoon finely chopped fresh parsley

In a large pot, bring 4 cups of salted water to a boil. Add 1 tablespoon of the olive oil, stir in the macaroni, and cook until al dente, about 7 minutes, or as directed on the package. Drain well and return to the pot.

Meanwhile, place a medium saucepan over medium heat and melt the butter. Add the shredded Muenster and ½ cup of the Cheddar by the handful and stir until melted. Add the salt, pepper, and milk. Lower the heat and stir until creamy. Mix in the flour and stir until the cheese starts to stick together.

Preheat the broiler. Remove the cheese mixture from the heat and gently stir into the macaroni until it is well coated. Spoon the macaroni mixture into an ungreased casserole dish and scatter the remaining shredded Cheddar on top. Place under the broiler about 6 inches from the heat source and broil until the top turns golden brown, about 3 minutes. Or, bake the macaroni, uncovered, at 350°F. for 30 minutes (but I recommend the broiler because it's faster and creates a crispier top). Sprinkle with chopped parsley, and allow to cool for a few minutes before serving.

roy's maui onion salad

Roy Yamaguchi, Hawaii's first recipient of the national James Beard Award and owner of the popular Roy's Restaurant, invented this recipe, which is full of exotic ingredients that are becoming more readily available in grocery stores across this country. There are a few suggested substitutes listed, just in case.

serves 4

1 small Maui or Vidalia onion, thinly sliced on a mandoline

1 large carrot, thinly sliced

4 ounces Japanese spice sprouts or sunflower sprouts, tops only, optional

½ Japanese or English hothouse cucumber, seeded and julienned

¼ cup pink pickled ginger

1 tablespoon canola oil

4 ounces mung bean sprouts

⅓ cup mirin (sweet rice wine)

¼ cup rice vinegar

2 tablespoons soy sauce

¼ cup bonito flakes

½ cup fresh yuzu or lime juice, or more to taste

2 teaspoons toasted white sesame seeds (see Note, page 69), for garnish

2 teaspoons black sesame seeds, for garnish

Juice of 1 lemon

Combine the onion, carrot, spice sprouts, cucumber, and pickled ginger in a mixing bowl. Heat the canola oil in a small sauté pan, and stir-fry the mung bean sprouts over high heat for 15 seconds. Add to the onion mixture. Set aside.

Combine the mirin, vinegar, soy sauce, and bonito flakes in a saucepan. Bring to a boil over medium heat. Remove from the heat and let the mixture steep and cool. Pour the sauce through a strainer into a bowl. Discard the bonito flakes and stir in the yuzu juice.

Divide the salad among 4 plates, sprinkle with the white and black sesame seeds and lemon juice, and spoon the sauce over everything.

geoffrey zakarian's town gingered cole slaw

Cole slaw works with just about any meal, and especially complements a hot burger on a nice spring day. Allowing the slaw to rest in the refrigerator for 30 minutes or so before serving will give the cabbage some time to absorb the other ingredients' flavors.

serves 4

½ **large head of savoy cabbage, cut into strips about ⅛ inch wide**

1 **medium carrot, peeled and sliced into a very fine julienne, 2-inch length**

1½ **teaspoons finely minced young ginger**

1½ **teaspoons finely minced garlic**

2 **tablespoons Mayonnaise (page 80)**

1 **tablespoon sherry vinegar**

½ **teaspoon kosher salt**

1 **pinch sugar**

1 **pinch freshly ground black pepper**

1 **tablespoon unsalted butter**

1½ **tablespoons golden raisins**

Combine the cabbage, carrot, ginger, garlic, mayonnaise, vinegar, salt, sugar, and pepper in a large bowl.

In a sauté pan over medium heat, lightly brown the butter and stir in the raisins. Cook and stir for 3 to 4 minutes. Add the warm raisins to the cole slaw. Check the seasoning, and refrigerate until ready to serve.

sautéed onions

I use sautéed onions in all sorts of dishes, from toppings for salads to burgers. You can vary this recipe in many ways (see Variations for a few), but the plain sautéed Vidalia onions have a mild sweet flavor all their own.

serves 4

1 **tablespoon olive oil**
2 **large Vidalia onions, peeled and sliced into very thin rings, preferably using a mandoline**
  Kosher salt to taste

Place a large skillet over medium heat. Add the olive oil and heat until it slides easily across the pan. Add the onions and salt. Cook until translucent and soft, stirring occasionally, for at least 7 minutes. To caramelize, keep cooking until golden brown, about 5 minutes more.

variations

While cooking onions add:

- A splash of Madeira wine.
- A splash of soy sauce and 2 pinches of sesame seeds.
- A pinch of curry power and a handful of golden raisins.
- A few tablespoons of pine nuts (also try toasting them separately before adding to the onions).

autumn bacon-apple potato salad

I love the combined flavors of warm apple, bacon, and raisins on a cool autumn day. Here, I add curry powder for some kick, though it may be omitted without compromising the outcome.

serves 6

15 small red potatoes, unpeeled and quartered

 1 small white onion, chopped

 2 teaspoons olive oil

½ teaspoon curry powder

 1 cup mayonnaise, preferably homemade (page 80)

½ Fuji apple, peeled and diced

 2 strips bacon, cooked crisp and crumbled

 2 tablespoons golden raisins

½ teaspoon freshly ground black pepper

 1 pinch salt, or to taste

In a large pot, boil the potatoes for 15 minutes. Drain and place in a large bowl. In a small skillet, cook the onion in the olive oil and curry powder over medium heat until tender, about 5 minutes. Combine with the potatoes. Add the remaining ingredients and gently mix until the potatoes are well coated. Chill before serving, or serve at room temperature fairly soon after making the salad.

josé's avocado ketchup

This recipe is somewhat similar to the traditional avocado dip, guacamole, except for the addition of tomatillos, which are available in many supermarkets in the tomato section. Often referred to as "the green cherry tomato," this vegetable is great fun to cook with because it adds a nice, sweet pungency.

yields 1½ cup

1 cup tomatillos, paper husks and stems removed, rinsed

2 ripe Hass avocados, peeled and pitted

1 medium garlic clove, peeled

¼ teaspoon freshly ground white pepper

¼ cup white vinegar

1 tablespoon sugar, or to taste

2 teaspoons kosher salt, or to taste

Place the shucked tomatillos in a saucepan with enough cold water just to cover. Bring to a boil, reduce the heat to low, and simmer for 5 minutes. Drain and place in the refrigerator until cool.

Using a blender, mix the tomatillos with the avocados, garlic, white pepper, vinegar, sugar, salt, and ¼ cup water until a smooth purée forms. Continue adding water until the mixture has the consistency of ketchup. Correct the sugar and salt to taste. Refrigerate for up to 1 week.

garden summer ketchup

When the garden is producing fresh tomatoes, onions, and peppers, try out this recipe. On a hot summer's day, it's particularly delightful.

yields 2 cups

- **2 large vine-ripened tomatoes, skins and seeds removed (see Note)**
- **6 ounces canned tomato paste**
- **½ cup light corn syrup**
- **⅓ cup white vinegar**
- **⅓ cup raisins, puréed in a food processor with ⅓ cup water**
- **1 tablespoon sugar**
- **3 tablespoons minced white onion**
- **3 tablespoons minced green pepper**
- **1 teaspoon kosher salt**
- **1 garlic clove, minced**

Place the tomatoes in a medium saucepan and squeeze them with your hands until they are well mashed. Add the tomato paste, corn syrup, white vinegar, raisin purée, ¼ cup water, sugar, onion, green pepper, salt, and garlic. Bring to a boil over medium-high heat for 5 minutes, stirring constantly. Reduce the heat to low and simmer for another 20 minutes, or until mixture thickens to your liking. Serve cooled. Refrigerate in a tightly covered container for up to 10 days.

tip: To skin a tomato, score an X on the end and remove the core. Place in boiling water for 30 seconds. Drain, cover with cold water, remove the tomato, and peel off the skin.

winter ketchup

Homemade ketchup makes all the difference and this recipe is prepared from start to finish in under 30 minutes.

yields 1½ cups

6 **ounces canned tomato paste**
½ **cup light corn syrup**
⅓ **cup white vinegar**
1 **tablespoon sugar**
1 **tablespoon white onion, minced**
1 **teaspoon kosher salt**
1 **pinch minced fresh garlic**

Combine all ingredients with ¼ cup of water in a medium saucepan. Bring to a boil over medium-high heat for 5 minutes, stirring constantly. Reduce the heat to low and cook for another 20 minutes, or until the mixture thickens to your liking (note that it will thicken further as it cools). Serve cooled. Refrigerate in a tightly covered container for up to 10 days.

dean fearing's burger buns

This recipe comes right from the source of great cooking, Chef Fearing. Try this and you'll find out why making buns from scratch is really worth the time and effort.

serves 12

½ **teaspoon granulated sugar**

1 **teaspoon active dry yeast**

4¼ **cups all-purpose flour**

½ **cup whole milk**

1 **large egg, at room temperature**

2 **tablespoons plus 1 teaspoon olive oil**

1 **teaspoon salt**

¼ **cup yellow cornmeal**

1 **large egg white**

In the bowl of an electric mixer, dissolve the sugar in 1½ cups plus 2 tablespoons warm water. Add the yeast and stir gently to dissolve. Allow the mixture to stand and foam for 6 to 8 minutes.

Add 4 cups of the flour, the milk, egg, 2 tablespoons of the olive oil, and the salt. With an electric mixer fitted with a dough hook, mix on slow speed for 1 minute, scraping down the sides of the bowl. Continue to mix on low until the dough forms a ball, about 4 to 5 minutes. If the dough attaches itself to the dough hook at any time, stop the mixer and pull the dough off the hook. (If a standing mixer is not available, follow the directions using a hand-held mixer, or knead by hand. The mixing times will increase depending on which alternative method is used.)

Knead the dough for 5 to 6 minutes on a clean, dry, lightly floured work surface, incorporating the remaining 1 teaspoon olive oil. Wipe out the mixing bowl with a warm, damp towel, return the dough to the bowl, and cover with the towel. Allow it to rise in a warm location until doubled in volume, about 2 hours.

Preheat the oven to 425°F. Place the dough on a lightly floured work surface. Punch down the dough. Use a sharp knife to cut the dough into 12 equal portions. Shape each dough portion into a ball. Flatten each dough ball into a ½-inch-thick disc. Place the flattened dough balls on a 15 × 10-inch baking sheet that has been sprinkled with the cornmeal. Cover the dough with a warm damp towel and allow it to rise in a warm location until doubled in size, about 45 minutes.

Whisk the egg white until foamy, and lightly brush over the flattened dough balls. With a sharp knife or razor blade, cut an X into the top of each dough ball. Bake for 12 to 14 minutes.

Allow the buns to cool thoroughly before slicing. The cooled buns may be frozen for several weeks in resealable plastic bags. Thaw the buns before grilling or toasting in the oven.

dean fearing's tobacco onion rings

Onion rings are lots of fun to fry, and make an excellent burger topping or side dish. These rings are sliced very thin with a spicy coating, producing a crispy onion lover's delight.

serves 4

5 cups peanut oil

3 cups all-purpose flour

1½ teaspoons cayenne pepper

1 tablespoon sweet paprika

1 teaspoon kosher salt

Several grinds of fresh black pepper

1 Spanish onion, peeled and sliced into very thin rings, preferably using a mandoline

1 red onion, peeled and sliced into very thin rings, preferably using a mandoline

Preheat the oven to 200°F.

Heat the oil in a deep-sided saucepan until it measures 350°F. on a candy or deep-fry thermometer.

In a shallow bowl, blend the flour, cayenne, paprika, salt, and black pepper. Separate the onion rings and dredge in the flour mixture, shaking off any excess. Carefully place in the hot oil, a few at a time, making sure they don't stick together. Fry for 3 to 5 minutes, or until golden brown.

Remove with a slotted spoon and drain briefly on paper towels. Place on a warm platter and keep warm in the low oven until all the onions are fried. Serve immediately.

acknowledgments

So many people helped make this book become a reality. Several of those provided incalculable support, including my husband, Bruce, who generously and tirelessly stands by me in all that I do; my wonderful daughters, Sienna Eve and Ava Jane, who pitched in and helped cook as well as simply behaved during the often exasperating process of writing a book; Annie Brito, for baby-sitting my kids so I could work without worry; my brother, John Gareis, Jr., for inspiring me to get into the culinary arts; my other siblings and their spouses, Donna and David Spielman, David and Amanda Gareis, and my sister and sister-in-law, Jennifer and Margarita, for listening to me prattle on about recipes and for enthusiastically trying my new dishes; my Sicilian grandmother, Josephine Concetta (a.k.a. Monga), for teaching me the importance of being a wife, granddaughter, mother, and cook; my in-laws, Bruce and Nancy Bent, for offering support and opinions, whether I asked for them or not; and my parents, John and Dolores, for teaching me how to successfully marry my two passions: family and food.

A special thanks to the chefs for their creative and delicious recipes—this book would not be complete without them. And to my neighbors, Michele and Ken Glassberg, who always opened their door to sample anything I sent their way.

Thanks to Michele Evans Plesser for encouraging me to take the next step; Greg Mowery for embracing and sending off my idea; Stacey Glick for taking on the project; Tom Steele for his infinite knowledge of the culinary arts and amazing ability to respond to an e-mail before I've written it; Ben Fink for providing mouthwatering photographs; Roscoe Bedsill for creating art from food; The Reserve Funds' staff for encouragement, especially Mary Belmonte, Eric Lansky, and Lisa Boone; and YC Media, for expecting big things from me.

I am especially grateful to Chris Pavone, my editor, whose insightful advice and strong vision acted as a guide while I was scrambling to deliver (on time!) my first manuscript.

And last but not least, a warm fuzzy thanks to my new puppies, Bingo and Daisy, for happily taking care of all the scraps.

index

conversion chart EQUIVALENT IMPERIAL AND METRIC MEASUREMENTS

American cooks use standard containers, the 8-ounce cup and a tablespoon that takes exactly 16 level fillings to fill that cup level. Measuring by cup makes it very difficult to give weight equivalents, as a cup of densely packed butter will weigh considerably more than a cup of flour. The easiest way therefore to deal with cup measurements in recipes is to take the amount by volume rather than by weight. Thus the equation reads:

1 cup = 240 ml = 8 fl. oz.   ½ cup = 120 ml = 4 fl. oz.

It is possible to buy a set of American cup measures in major stores around the world.

In the States, butter is often measured in sticks. One stick is the equivalent of 8 tablespoons. One tablespoon of butter is therefore the equivalent to ½ ounce/15 grams.

LIQUID MEASURES

Fluid Ounces	U.S.	Imperial	Milliliters
	1 teaspoon	1 teaspoon	5
¼	2 teaspoons	1 dessertspoon	10
½	1 tablespoon	1 tablespoon	14
1	2 tablespoons	2 tablespoons	28
2	¼ cup	4 tablespoons	56
4	½ cup		110
5		¼ pint or 1 gill	140
6	¾ cup		170
8	1 cup		225
9			250, ¼ liter
10	1¼ cups	½ pint	280
12	1½ cups		340
15		¾ pint	420
16	2 cups		450
18	2¼ cups		500, ½ liter
20	2½ cups	1 pint	560
24	3 cups		675
25		1¼ pints	700
27	3½ cups		750
30	3¾ cups	1½ pints	840
32	4 cups or 1 quart		900
35		1¾ pints	980
36	4½ cups		1000, 1 liter
40	5 cups	2 pints or 1 quart	1120

SOLID MEASURES

U.S. and Imperial Measures		Metric Measures	
Ounces	Pounds	Grams	Kilos
1		28	
2		56	
3½		100	
4	¼	112	
5		140	
6		168	
8	½	225	
9		250	¼
12	¾	340	
16	1	450	
18		500	½
20	1¼	560	
24	1½	675	
27		750	¾
28	1¾	780	
32	2	900	
36	2¼	1000	1
40	2½	1100	
48	3	1350	
54		1500	1½

OVEN TEMPERATURE EQUIVALENTS

Fahrenheit	Celsius	Gas Mark	Description
225	110	¼	Cool
250	130	½	
275	140	1	Very Slow
300	150	2	
325	170	3	Slow
350	180	4	Moderate
375	190	5	
400	200	6	Moderately Hot
425	220	7	Fairly Hot
450	230	8	Hot
475	240	9	Very Hot
500	250	10	Extremely Hot

Any broiling recipes can be used with the grill of the oven, but beware of high-temperature grills.

EQUIVALENTS FOR INGREDIENTS

all-purpose flour—plain flour
baking sheet—oven tray
buttermilk—ordinary milk
cheesecloth—muslin
coarse salt—kitchen salt
cornstarch—cornflour

eggplant—aubergine
granulated sugar—caster sugar
half and half—12% fat milk
heavy cream—double cream
light cream—single cream
parchment paper—greaseproof paper

plastic wrap—cling film
scallion—spring onion
shortening—white fat
unbleached flour—strong, white flour
zest—rind
zucchini—courgettes or marrow